# The Best-Loved Game

# The Best-Loved Game

## One Summer of English Cricket

by

GEOFFREY MOORHOUSE

HODDER AND STOUGHTON
LONDON   SYDNEY   AUCKLAND   TORONTO

British Library Cataloguing in Publication Data
Moorhouse, Geoffrey
  The best-loved game
  1. Cricket – England – History – 20th century
  I. Title
  796.358'0942          GV928.G7

  ISBN 0 340 24147 0

To
Jane and Andrew,
Brigid and Michael,
Marilyn and Sam

Who also watched

# Contents

# Introduction

THIS BOOK OWES SOMETHING TO MR KERRY PACKER, without whom it might not have been written. I don't believe I'd heard of him until the 1977 cricket season started in England, and the news broke that he had secretly been enlisting international players to perform in his employment for larger salaries than they had ever known in their lives. It soon became apparent, in the course of that year, that a great conflict of interest had arisen in cricket. At the very least it was a conflict between Mr Packer and the players in his pay, on the one hand, and the traditional cricketing authorities on the other. The repercussions of this, in England alone, have already included an action in the High Court which has cost the authorities a lot of money in legal fees and gained them nothing that they had sought. The conflict has also meant the disappearance from our cricket of Tony Greig, who captained England in the Centenary Test against Australia in 1977, a match which was thought by everyone who watched it to be an exemplary exhibition of the sport. I do not wish to argue here the rights and wrongs of the Packer affair, much less to recount its already wearisome history. I will say only that, as I write this with the 1978 season over and done, a working party of the Test and County Cricket Board has recommended that next year all county cricketers should be paid a minimum basic wage of £4,000, and I don't think that's nearly good enough for what they give us in return. But the pages that follow have been written out of a deep affection for a form of cricket that has evolved without Mr Packer's sudden interest in its future, and out of a fear that it might be changed for the worse if Mr Packer's attitude to the game were to prevail. It seemed important to record an English season while the matter was still in balance, lest the shape and nature of our cricket should presently be spoiled.

I first fell under the spell of cricket as every other small boy will have done, by batting and bowling on the nearest available space the moment I got home from school. With the other lads of the village, I used to spend hours in the field beside our house with a rubber ball and a home-made bat, whose handle was fashioned from an old carpet beater, with a bicycle inner tube rolled double down to the shoulder of the blade, which had once been a mahogany shelf. I first saw professional cricketers play in a charity match down in the town towards the end of the war. Eddie Paynter batted in that game, a legend in our part of the world and only just past his great days. So did E. R. Conradi, later to become a Cambridge Blue. And there were three great West Indians – Martindale, Achong and St Hill – who probably impressed me with their colour as much as by their skill, for almost certainly they were the first black men I'd ever seen. I cannot, alas, remember anything else of that match, though many times since I've tried to recall how it went. But I know that, after that, I went looking for cricket to watch. I found it mostly in the Lancashire leagues to start with but, when 1946 came, I entered Old Trafford for the first time. It was a lovely sun-hazed day and the county ground seemed enormously grand, and Alf Gover was bowling with that curious cocktail shaker action to Washbrook and Place. I sat there entranced, hoping it would never end: and, in a sense, it never has.

I must not exaggerate my feeling for the game. I don't suppose I've played more than a dozen times since I left school, and I haven't been a cricket writer since my prentice days as a journalist in the North of England and New Zealand. There are many things in life much more important than any sport, even this one, which stirs me more than any other I have known. The compelling attraction of cricket, however, is that it manifests so much of what is more important in life than its purely athletic qualities, which are themselves sophisticated develop-ments of essentially primitive human skills. Like the human condition at large, it is very complex and infinitely subtle, and even when it is played most belligerently it contains a great deal of warmth that has been generated by its past. It has also embodied certain values that are too often sneered at now, to do with what is fair and what is not, what is generous and what is intolerably mean. In *Beyond a Boundary*, that classic piece of writing on the game and much else, C. L. R. James said that "All sneering at these (values) as cant or hypocrisy is ignorance or stupidity." And I believe him to be right.

Two examples of cricket's most precious spirit will suffice. On the second day of the Lord's Test in 1975, seven Australian wickets had fallen for 81, and all England was cockahoop because we had the old enemy on the run. Ross Edwards then stayed put for three hours and gradually brought Australia back into the game, until Woolmer had him leg before. When that wicket fell, our roar of triumph and relief was probably heard a couple of miles away. But then, as Edwards started to walk, we realised what an awful thing had happened. He'd missed his century by a solitary run, and no man had ever deserved a century more than Ross Edwards that day. So we stood up, nearly 30,000 of us, and applauded him all the way back; and so did every member of the England team. Almost two years later, in Melbourne, Randall of Nottinghamshire had scored 161 in the last innings of the Centenary Test when he was given out for a catch at the wicket off Chappell. As the Englishman turned to go, Rodney Marsh, one of the most combative players the game has known, pointed out to the umpire that his catch had not been a clean one; and Randall was recalled to continue an innings that might have won the match for England.

It is this spirit, perhaps above everything else, that sent me round the cricket fields of England to write about the season of 1978. I went as a cricket watcher who can rarely find time to see more than a single day's play of any match, not as a cricket reporter who covers games in full. Although I attach the completed score to every piece I've written here, some of the first-class matches continued after I'd left. The longest piece is about a meeting between Northants and Worcester, which I saw from first ball to last because I wanted to track the distinctive rhythms of the three-day match. I wrote as I went along and I have changed nothing since, so that observations were once or twice overtaken by subsequent events; they should be read with an eye on the date of that particular match. Most of the cricket I saw, in fact, lasted no more than a single day. This was partly due to the weather we didn't much enjoy last summer, which cut so many matches short. But it was also a matter of choice, because this is not a collection of pieces about the first-class game. It is an attempt to reflect English cricket in general, the people who play it and the people who watch, the background from which it springs and the elements which give it life. I have simply hoped to convey why cricket is for me, and for vast numbers all over the world, not only the most absorbing but the best-loved game.

# Opening Day at Lord's

*April 19*                                              *Lord's*
## MCC v MIDDLESEX

THERE IS A RITUAL FOR THE OPENING OF THE CRICKET season and it always begins by getting there early. Children feel like this on Christmas morning, and I certainly don't intend to miss a minute of my own most eagerly awaited day of the year. The old chap on point duty at the Grace Gates is unseasonably lugubrious, even for 9.45 in weather as grey and chill as this. "No idea when we'll be opening," he says, "until They tell us. We've been having a lot of rain lately." There was a time when I would have snorted at this genuflection towards the masters of Lord's, but I have lately become much less irritated by the loftiness of Them, since Mr Packer introduced the infinitely less congenial concept of Him. So I bide my time equably, with two young autograph hunters and a patient Scot who is sensibly dressed as for a withering day at Carnoustie. An hour before play is due to start, They decide to let us in, and we rush through those gates as though ten thousand others were also bent on reaching the nets first. There will be time later on to sniff out the familiarities of the dear old place, to see how it has weathered this past winter of cricketing discontents. The first thing, always, is to hasten to the Nursery and watch the cricketers working out, to hear that first heady tock of a ball upon a bat.

There are maybe twenty of us to appraise the initial rite of spring. Middlesex are fiercely at it already, but we are having trouble recognising some. An elderly gent in an MCC tie sidles up in that casual way we net-watchers have. "Who's that blighter in the beard? Selvey, d'ye think? Doesn't look big enough in the backside for him." The tone is speculative, the sentiment not meant to be rude. We are like a pair of racegoers, sizing up bloodstock in the ring. Selvey it is who is hurling them down. Gatting plays one on to his ankle, lets out a howl of pain and limps off for repairs. Jones, not playing today but here all the same, gasps loudly with the effort of delivering each ball, though it sounds more as if he's telling the batsman to take that. At the MCC nets, the spring-heeled Hendrick is wheeling them up to Botham, whose arrival has been accompanied by a television camera and its crew. A short, brick-faced fellow has ranged himself behind the Somerset man as Botham shapes up for the first practice ball, and announces to a companion that, in his opinion, this is a much overrated player. Botham stoops to pick Hendrick's inswinger from the back of the net and the two cricketers grin at each other; but perhaps they haven't heard. The rest of us grin faintly, too, for it is even good to be again within earshot of the season's first oracle. We are all quietly that, of course, as we dawdle in clusters behind each set of stumps, watching closely the dip and swing of balls through the air, certain how a delivery should be played before the batsman makes his move. We suck our teeth, critically, when he snicks one up off the edge, and we shake our heads ruefully when cold fingers let fly a long hop. I don't reckon much to the synthetic gleam on all these bats, myself, with deep furrows and worse gouged out of their backs. I sniff the air in vain for a trace of linseed oil and am saddened by this inorganic growth of poly-awfulised willow.

As the players begin to move away from the nets we, too, drift off, for there are things to take in before we can comfortably settle down to the play. A pause at the bookshop to pick up the new Wisden which no one, thank God, has yet sought to revamp, though I dearly wish its index could be reorganised one day on logical lines. A wander round the back of the stands after that, and there must be a hundred or more people on the ground by now. There will, of course, be the annual smirk from the evening papers at the thinness of the opening day crowd, but one of the attractions of this day is that all these athletes perform on it for this handful of us: eighteenth-century princelings were not served better when great musicians came to court to play for their benefit alone. I am very content to be one of this highly privileged few, with that flaring bank of red tulips in full bloom behind "Q" Stand, and the herbaceous borders of the Memorial Garden neatly trimmed for our benefit alone. This is the day to pop into the museum to reassure yourself that the Ashes are still safely there, and the sparrow shot down by Jahangir Khan's medium pace in 1936, and Pelham Warner's well-oiled bat thickly bound (what's more) with pink adhesive tape; and all the rest of our priceless heirlooms and marvellous bric-à-brac. Later in the season, when the big crowds come, Lord's will be surrendered to nearly as much push and shove as an American baseball park, and in that way will not be quite so much fun at all. Today it is quietly brooding, almost rurally so, as it waits for its season to begin.

Nothing seems to have changed since last September, apart from the completion of the indoor cricket school. The benches at the front of the Mound Stand are still warped and lacking a fresh coat of paint. Conrad Ritblat is still advertising from the balcony of the Grandstand. The green of the pitch is still flecked with faint patches of beige, lingering residue of the 1976 drought. When the bell tolls, just before the umpires walk out, it still suggests campanology, as though Grandsire Triples might shortly be the order of the day. Two old ladies just behind me are wisely tucking car rugs round their knees and our oracle (again within earshot) is declaring that the pitch doesn't look too hard to him. Frank Hayes has evidently decided that it is green enough to give some movement off the seam for, having won the toss, he has put the 1977 joint champions in to bat. The MCC players come down the pavilion steps unhurriedly, as though reluctant to commit themselves to a day like this. There is not much wind, but there doesn't need to be under this glum sky; you can feel the cold air on your cheeks just by slowly walking along. A spatter of clapping as MCC take the field behind their boyish skipper. This is a very young team and even Hayes (at thirty-one easily the oldest of them) remains the perpetual youth with a flaxen early-Beatle mop. He sets his field, on his first outing as a captain, with thumbs-up signs, expressive long-range winks and nods. It looks as if Lancashire are going to be led this season in an extremely matey fashion, from alongside rather than from in front or above. The clapping, prompted by the pavilion, becomes a little louder as Mike Brearley follows MCC out, to play his first innings since breaking an arm in Karachi three months ago. He still conveys the eccentric under that strange, protective headgear of his, as though he had absent-mindedly put his cap on when already wearing something else.

There is a moment of pause at the start of a cricket season, when the field is still settling down, when the opening bowler is yet again going back to his mark after two or three run-ups, when the striker may or may not be taking stance in earnest, when we in the seats are still dreamily absorbed by too many details in this gradual process of renewal, trying to watch half a dozen things at once. It is not until Hendrick is almost up to the stumps, and still going full out, that one realises the game has actually begun. By the end of that maiden over I am quite unable to recall whether Brearley played the first ball, or whether it went through to Downton standing well back. A neat, slim lad, the new Kent wicketkeeper. He paws the ground with a foot between balls, does a bit of toe-touching to loosen up, but there is nothing like the eurhythmic displays of Alan Knott. Doesn't wear a cap, either; doesn't need to on such a miserable day. After his first delivery from the Nursery end, Stevenson reaches for the sawdust. Mike Smith (another Middlesex man who's spent his winter growing a beard) puts his fifth ball away to square leg for 2. The first runs of the season are on the board.

The ritual would be disturbed if the start were not painstakingly slow; time enough for headlong cricket later on, when we have properly digested this first appetising day. In my early years on the *Manchester Guardian* (it was still that, then) there was a passage in the style book which frowned upon the excessive use of superlatives in word or mood. "We don't want to give the impression," the Editor wrote, "that we live in a perpetual state of excitement." I'm not sure that A. P. Wadsworth was ever a cricket enthusiast, but he ought to have been with that cast of mind. Cricket would be just another exhibition of high athletic skills, if it were not for its singular grace and its profoundly human character. Perpetual excitement would be an impediment to a proper appreciation of these; we need the slow periods – just now and again – to reflect on the character of this game and to savour fully the richness of its nature. Eight runs in the first half hour this morning are therefore acceptable enough. Later in the season I shall doubtless quibble, but not at Lord's on opening day. Brearley is trying to reconstruct his fortunes out there, cautiously playing himself back into shape. The newly-bearded Smith is taking his time, another Drake letting us all wait before he makes his move. The MCC players are simply trying to keep warm, and I don't envy those slips with their fingers frozen stiff. Up in the pavilion balconies, topcoats and newspapers are about evenly distributed in this waiting time. Our oracle on the Mound Stand keeps his circulation on the move by endless talk. At 11.30 it's "Hit the ball, man. All these blokes are taught today is how to defend." At noon it's a depressing review of bad weather all over the world; ". . . they've been having typhoons in Western Australia and in San Francisco the other day it was so freezing the cables on the cable cars snapped. It's sun spots, you know, that's what's causing it." We could do with a few of those this morning at Lord's.

The pace does quicken, by and by. Brearley and Smith begin to move from a shuffle to a walk, with a hint that before long they might contemplate a jog. The 50 comes up within an hour and a half ("They've been lucky to have been put in today. I wouldn't have put them in. There's no bounce in the pitch, I mean.") and shortly afterwards Hayes tries a bit of spin. The sun breaks through the overcast as Graveney takes over from the pavilion end on legs like stilts, bearing the ball to his delivery as though carefully carrying a handful of sawdust. Two overs later, in

17

order to swap ends, he gives way to Jesty and the Hampshire medium-pacer has Smith caught and bowled first ball. Brearley by now has his innings well founded, is beginning to thump the ball sweetly through the covers. Twice in one over, Stevenson has a long chase to the rails just in front of us and seems thankful for the exercise, even though we now have sun. He flings the ball full-pitch into Downton's gloves and grins happily at his own expertise. I believe I have seen that cheerful, perky face before, across innumerable fish-and-chip counters back home in the north. What with the sun and that first wicket of the season, we are all now in pretty good heart. We have been joined by perhaps a couple of hundred other spectators and some of them are daring enough to try the beer and the powdered tea-with-milk they serve at the Tavern bars. The oracle delivers a final homily: "I once saw Wally Hammond put two consecutive balls over that sightscreen. You never see that nowadays. Straight, mind you, not over by the clock." He departs for lunch and we do not see him again. Halfway through the afternoon it occurs to me that perhaps the Tavern's fluids have claimed their first victim of the season.

The afternoon begins in something approaching warmth and reaches high excitement. Brearley coverdrives Botham for 4 to get his 50 and the applause is accompanied by the sound of an ambulance hooting hysterically down St John's Wood Road. Botham's next ball is a shameful long hop, Brearley's stroke is an astonished swish, and Downton takes the catch with so little fuss that for a moment it isn't clear which fielder in the arc behind has snapped it up. Botham roars like a bull, flings his arms high and wide but doesn't, on this occasion, about-turn in mid-air to appeal to the umpire. His all-round talents include a thespian skill and even if he never makes another Wally Hammond it seems possible that he might fill at least one gap left by Fred Trueman. The day, though, is about to be his. From 102 for 1, Middlesex will tumble to 105 for 5 and Botham will have taken all four wickets in the crash, pulling off the first hat-trick of his career on the way. At 2.55 he bowls Radley's off-stump when the batsman plays back instead of coming forward. Botham does the same thing with his next ball, Barlow being in his characteristic matador pose with elbow high, body erect and chin sunk on chest. The MCC players meet in a mid-wicket coven around the beaming Botham, while Barlow walks back and Gatting, at the other end, talks to Cecil Cook and fiddles with the strapping of his pads. On the Mound Stand we have become wide-eyed and very intent, nodding agreeably to each other while we wait and see. On the pavilion balconies, every newspaper has been put aside. When Featherstone comes in, while he is taking guard, Botham is walking back to his mark, a sense of purpose in every step he takes. He spits aggressively just before he gets to his turn, waits, spits again, and begins to move into his run. The whole ground is totally concentrated as he breaks into those long bounding strides, as he flings himself into the final action of release. Then our eyes whip to the other end and we roar with delight. Featherstone got the bottom of his bat somewhere in the way, but his middle stump is tilted back and he has been perfectly yorked. The MCC team rush like sparrows from a hedge to surround the bowler and he, beside himself with joy, is showing them how it was done with vigorous darts-player gestures of his right arm. When the exuberance subsides, when Botham turns to walk back again to his mark, Gatting steps quietly forward and shakes him by the hand. And I suddenly feel soppy about this lovely, generous game. Two years ago I was obliged to watch a season of baseball in the States, and it had its glorious moments, too: but I never saw an opponent do a simple thing like that.

Edmonds goes a few minutes later, to Cook's catch off Miller, but it is Botham who appeals so loudly that Arthur Jepson has to wait a few seconds for his head to clear before making up his mind. Gatting and Gould manage to halt this Middlesex collapse with a sturdy, grafting stand, but then the innings goes into its final decline. Graveney takes the pair of them, with balls lobbed over like hand-grenades. Stevenson's hard work is rewarded by

Selvey's wicket. Botham bowls Emburey, first delivery with the new ball. His team-mates clap him into the pavilion, and once again he has riveted spectators with five wickets in an innings. The sun vanishes and MCC are soon batting in the same sort of gloom that began the day; heaven knows why Edmonds is wearing his white beach hat, which seems an even greater affectation than usual in this light. Cook, preferring the regulation maroon cap of his county, seems ill at ease and does not stay long before Gould takes him behind off an uncertain stroke to Selvey. Gower lasts longer and promises more before he fatally raises his head and clumps a ball in a convenient curve to where Featherstone has enough time to stand his ground and wait for it to drop. Love, meanwhile, has been showing signs of a do; a very self-contained young man I think, not given to conversation with his colleagues nearby in the gully and slips. He is batting with concentration, too, and rips a beautiful boundary straight past the bowler along the ground, the ball being almost up to the sightscreen before anybody else has moved.

My eye, though, is on Frank Hayes. I have known no English batsman as elegant as him since Tom Graveney was in his prime, and for this reason alone I have wished him to become secure in England's team. Will he return again this season, with an opening so obviously there, and this time manage to hold his place? He hooks the first ball he gets and, although it falls short of Selvey on our boundary, I hold my breath and wish he weren't quite so cavalier. He takes the hint of his near-miss and plays quietly after that, but with confidence in all his strokes. He has a word with Love in the middle a couple of times and from his gestures seems to be telling the Yorkshireman, now well into his stride, to get on with it and not to mind if he pinches most of the bowling. Maybe this season's captaincies will help Hayes to do justice to himself at last. He is desperately unlucky to be out a few minutes later. He plays the meticulous defensive stroke that was a trademark of Bert Sutcliffe's craft; body stretched right forward, front leg jack-knifed, back leg braced, head over the shoulder of the bat, blade low and all but parallel to the ground. It is a stroke which, ninety-nine times out of a hundred, stuns the ball instantly into the turf. This time the ball flies off at an angle and it has surely flown safely low. But from the Mound Stand we see Gatting lunge full-length across the grass at silly mid-on, the other Middlesex fielders jumping with astonishment, clapping their hands in reflexes of surprise. And Frank Hayes, alas, is out. Had he stayed another five minutes the umpires would have come to his aid, for the light has been getting worse and, twenty minutes before time, they call a halt to opening day.

No matter; we cannot feel cheated after a day like this. Brearley has come home with half a century. Downton has scarcely let anything pass. Love has looked as if he might make a lasting mark. All this and Botham's hat-trick, too. The most important thing, though, is that cricket has begun again. For all the frictions that may this season inflame the politics of the game, a healing balm is about to spread across the land.

## MIDDLESEX—*First Innings*

| | |
|---|---:|
| J. M. BREARLEY c Downton b Botham | 51 |
| M. J. SMITH c and b Jesty | 35 |
| C. T. RADLEY, b Botham | 13 |
| M. W. GATTING c Downton b Graveney | 23 |
| G. D. BARLOW b Botham | 0 |
| N. G. FEATHERSTONE b Botham | 0 |
| P. H. EDMONDS c Cook b Miller | 1 |
| I. J. GOULD lbw Graveney | 24 |
| J. E. EMBUREY b Botham | 2 |
| M. W. W. SELVEY b Stevenson | 11 |
| R. HERKES not out | 0 |
| Extras (b 1, lb 2, nb 4) | 7 |
| Total | 167 |

Fall of wickets: 67, 102, 105, 105, 105, 106, 146, 154, 167
Bowling: HENDRICK 17–8–27–0; STEVENSON 18–4–53–1;
BOTHAM 17.3–5–43–5; GRAVENEY 18–10–23–2; JESTY 3–2–3–1;
MILLER 12–6–11–1.

## MCC — *First Innings*

| | |
|---|---:|
| D. I. GOWER c Featherstone b Selvey | 12 |
| G. COOK c Gould b Selvey | 5 |
| J. D. LOVE not out | 22 |
| F. C. HAYES c Gatting b Edmonds | 6 |
| T. E. JESTY not out | 0 |
| Extras | 0 |
| | |
| Total (for 3) | 45 |

Fall of wickets: 12, 22, 45.

Bowling: SELVEY 7–2–22–2; HERKES 5–3–9–0; GATTING 3–0–14–0;
EDMONDS 2–2–0–1.

Did not bat: G. Miller, I. T. Botham, G. B. Stevenson,
D. A. Graveney, P. R. Downton, M. Hendrick.

Umpires: C. Cook and A. Jepson.

No further play was possible on the remaining two days
because of rain.

# Young Gentlemen v Players

ANYONE WHO GOES TO FENNER'S BEFORE APRIL IS OUT DOES so at some risk to his health. They can be enjoying an early heat wave at Lord's, and even old Trafford, Buxton and Headingley may be basking in sunny days. But Cambridge in the spring is likely to be scoured by winds from the east that have swept unhindered across the Hundred Foot Drain, the Bedford Level and the Great North Fen. I have chosen to be here so early in the season because I have wished to be sure of seeing Procter at least once again. It is true that Gloucestershire have made him captain for another year after his winter's work in Mr Packer's camp, but that is no longer the insurance policy it used to be before this wretched turning point in the allegiances of the game. Already, Nottinghamshire have ejected Rice from both captaincy and club, with the county championship not yet begun, and the only surety there seems to be the wholly miserable one of litigation yet to come. Better risk catching cold at Fenner's, then, for a certain sight of the South African's all-round skills: but what a reason for going to watch a cricket match!

It is deeply ironic that I have come to a stronghold of the old amateur game on this occasion, largely because professional cricket has got itself into such a mess. Not that we should delude ourselves about the texture of university cricket these days, with several of the young gentlemen in this Cambridge side already on county books and therefore able to anticipate paid playing careers the moment their studies are done. And to hark back

23

nostalgically to the grand old amateur days, with dis-
paraging sniffs about professionalism in sport, usually
means begging a lot of questions about bread and butter,
and the way some lucky lads never had to rely on their
cricket to provide it. All the same, there was something I
esteem embedded in the amateur's game, a nonchalance
that no professional can ever really afford. More often
than not, perhaps, this was an irritating bore, especially to
the professionals who played in the same teams. Richard
Barlow must sometimes have got pretty fed up with his
carefree Hornby long ago, particularly when that
fox-hunting gent caused the old pro to be run out (as
often happened) with consequent damage to his batting
average and therefore to his prospects of trade. But from
time to time the nonchalance of the amateur included
such a modesty about his own worth that it was a
genuinely noble thing.

As I tack through the undergraduate flow of bicycles on
my way to the ground, I catch myself wondering what on
earth Charles Studd would have thought of cricket's
present plight. He made a century and took 5 wickets in
one innings when Cambridge defeated the Australians in
1882, subsequently captained the university and played
five times for England against our greatest cricketing foe.
Twice, in those years, he did the double of 1,000 runs and
100 wickets. And then he turned his back on it all. Having
been roused by the Evangelical fervour of Moody and
Sankey's student crusade, he became a missionary when
he went down, spent the rest of his life in Africa and the
East, and never played cricket again. What, indeed,
would a more recent Cambridge ghost have reckoned
about our present obsession with the financial rewards of
the game? When I started watching first-class cricket a
balding man in specs, who used to crouch behind the
Fenner's stumps, was wicket-keeping for England. He
toured Australia in Hammond's post-war side, with
Godfrey Evans chosen as his Number Two. He was noted
in the scorecards of his county, Yorkshire, as P. A. Gibb,
to distinguish him from the paid cricketers in the side (like
Hutton, L. and Coxon, A.) and many years later he was to

coach the young Mike Procter at his school in Durban. But Paul Gibb's old and precious amateur status never served him as well in the world as it did others of the teaching, the landowning and the stockbrocking clan. When he died, last December, he was working as a bus driver down Guildford way, and he was completely overlooked by Wisden in its otherwise all-embracing obituaries of 1977.

Some things change very little, though. It is something of a relief to find that they are still setting up type for the scorecards in the printery behind the scoreboard some time after play has begun (and when these appear, Procter's name is spelt with a penultimate "o", the compositor perhaps being too well disciplined in university ways). It has turned out not such a bad day after all, with no great wind blasting down from The Wash. Nippy enough, though, to make Procter decide to bat, so that his men can spend as much time as possible in the pavilion warmth. Some of them defer that pleasure, taking to the nets as soon as Stovold and Tait start their day's work in the middle, though it is not at once obvious that those are Gloucestershire players practising in the far corner of the ground, for they have been camouflaged and I suspect some sponsor's gaudy brand. They wear uniform trousers of dark blue, and strange-looking tops that seem to have been designed by the man who thought up the tailplane livery for British Airways. This may improve the appearance of a Trident, but it makes county cricketers look like the chorus line from an economy-class production of "The Student Prince". I do not like it, and I hope our new patronising masters will soon know where to stop.

Out in the middle, where the cricketers are properly dressed, the difference between the established professionals and the up and coming lads is at once apparent. Stovold, as thickly muffled as a polar bear, has several seasons behind him now and it shows in the ease with which he is playing this Cambridge attack. He is soon hooking and driving without difficulty and, when Greig just once raps him on the pads and tries an appeal, it is distinctly an event. But at the other end Tait, a young newcomer to the side, looks as if life is exceedingly hard. He gropes forward a lot, seems uncertain how the ball is coming off the pitch, misses several times and enjoys one great slice of luck. He swings defiantly at Howat and snicks the ball head-high just wide of the stumps; but Littlewood's goalkeeping dive has taken off a fraction too late and the ball is almost at the boundary before it is stopped.

In the first hour 52 runs are scored, and Stovold is ahead by well over 2 to 1. By this time, though, Tait has discovered that there is little to worry about in the pitch itself. Cambridge wickets are not quite the blissful batting strips Cyril Coote prepared once upon a time, when young May and young Sheppard and young Doggart and their peers each got a bucketful of runs almost every time he went in: it is nearly thirty years since the university and West Indies between them scored 1,324 runs for only 7 wickets in the course of three days. The bowler who opens at Fenner's now need not feel hopeless before he even starts, though against class batsmen he may well be footsore and very thirsty by the end of a day. Tait, realising that the ball almost invariably comes through at a predictable height, settles more confidently into his play and, just before lunch, Stovold is the first to go. Having muddied several Cambridge flannels by causing out-fielders to slide frantically across the grass, he pulls one more delivery high towards the long leg boundary. But this time Peck gets there before the ball complete its arc and he takes it low, on yet another blackened knee. That blow might have made Stovold's 50 and he ambles very slowly back. The pavilion's warmth is not quite so tempting now; the sun has found a way through the fenny mists overhead so that, when Zaheer comes out, the rims of his glasses glint and the gold charm around his neck twinkles as he walks.

Tait keeps going steadily for some time after the break until he mis-hits Allbrook's off-spin and Hignell catches him smartly at silly mid-on. The stage is thus set for a classic batting display with Zaheer at one end, Procter at the other, against bowling that has been steady but lacking in guile. The play will now also embody every conceivable irony that has been built into cricket today. Pakistani and South African, brown man and white, standing together, defying all the rest. Not just professionals against amateurs, but two Packer employees facing a team who are here (nominally at least) mostly for the fun. Two highly paid men who, in their Packer season, will have become accustomed to playing on almost empty grounds, which is not much different from Fenner's today except that Mr Packer's games were rather expensive to watch, whereas nobody in Cambridge has had to pay a penny to get in. Yet the ironies do not matter this afternoon, being reduced to their proper scale by the latent skills of those two batsmen out there. I am not the only person who becomes more intent at the prospect of drama about to begin. The old fellows sharing my bench along the wall stop talking, drift into monosyllables, are finally quiet as Procter walks out to bat. The man who hangs the numbers on the scoreboard bends to pick up a fresh square of tin, knowing that he will surely need it before this over is out. It is not that Zaheer alone hasn't already been hitting the ball; he has. But with the two of them there, harder work is at hand. A young man who has been walking his Labrador round the ground stops in front of the vacant seats by the tennis courts and bids the dog stay. I can't imagine why, at this moment, the gutty plop of tennis should still be heard over that hedge; perhaps someone ought to tell them that Procter has just joined Zaheer. If it comes to that, shouldn't someone inform the people in those new dwellings at the far end? They have the best domestic view of cricket I have ever seen, open-space windows within a few feet of the boundary rope revealing bookcases galore, modish chandeliers and all the other home comforts that Harrods or John Lewis can provide. But (what a shocking waste) not a face has been visible since this morning's play began.

Hignell, Gloucestershire player too, sets his field carefully, mindful of both batsmen's ways. Procter looks at it briefly, has seen it all before. His bat is well blotched with pink and not one mark appears to be anywhere near the edge. He doesn't even bother to stand still when an early appeal splits the air, knowing better than Allbrook himself that it was made purely on spec. He sweeps the next ball for 4 and, this time, nobody has moved until the ball is across the line. Three or four more shots and he reaches 13 with a vicious square cut for 4 to the car park off Gardiner. At this point he takes off one of his sweaters, though the Cambridge fielders still look a bit pinched in two apiece. It is an illusion, of course, but the bowlers do not seem to be releasing as much energy in run-up, delivery and follow-through, as Procter is doing by merely batting at a crease. Most of his runs are coming in boundaries so forcefully struck that the outfielders need only trot to retrieve the ball from the perimeters of the gound; and the infielders stand splayed, hugging their hands beneath their armpits in the breeze. It is this carefully controlled power in Procter's batting that seizes the attention most. He sends the ball in one bound against the beer tent with a cross-batted heave that may not be recommended in the coaching manuals but which has every muscle in his body launched tremendously into the striking of that ball; and his eye has taken care of any defiance of the rules. The next ball is clouted along the ground over the long-on boundary. The one after that is turned into the gully for a single, with a punching movement of the wrists. Next over he drives another 4 to mid-wicket. He looks as though he could go on like this for the rest of the day. But then he straight drives at a ball from Greig, beautifully following through with the stroke. No good guessing from my angle what went wrong, but Littlewood has taken a catch behind and Procter is out. He has been there for much less than an hour, scoring three runs for every two from his companion, to make 30, and in every sense he has dominated the play.

While he and Zaheer were together the difference between the highest class of batsman and the good county player was apparent in the time each man made for himself before he actually struck the ball. Scarcely a delivery reached them without either being ready and waiting to make what then seemed the perfectly obvious stroke, the mark of high talent being that it looked so certain to be made, so obvious when it was done, not needing the swift reflex that allows the batsman to change his mind with the ball already on the way. Otherwise, the contrast between the Pakistani and the South African was great, the graceful power of Procter set against the gentle aggressions of Zaheer. Procter looked as if he was going to give every ball he hit every ounce of his strength; Zaheer seems to be letting slender arms do most of the work. A much slimmer man, so that one is more conscious of his body's flow as it moves towards the ball. When he strikes a boundary, as he does quite a lot today, it is in a rippling motion that has begun in the region of his feet, spread languidly up legs and trunk, more swiftly along the arms, and not ended until the ball is well despatched, with the batsman still perfectly balanced in the composure of his completed stroke. Occasionally he misses, straightens up, throws his dark head back and grimaces at the sky, gestures with his right hand as though weighing something in the palm. But Zaheer isn't missing much on this brightening afternoon.

Hignell switches his bowlers from end to end in his efforts to break through again, but Zaheer plays all of them almost as he will. Once Greig leaps to his right, agile as his brother, to take the Pakistani off his own bowling, but can only manage to paw the ball to the ground. Allbrook pays for that one with two 4s hit off successive balls in the next over. When Procter was with him, Zaheer had sent Gardiner for 6 near the tennis court hedge, which excited the watchful Labrador no end. Now he hauls Howat square to the other side of the ground, where the ball lands full toss on the roof of a car. The owner gets out to inspect the damage, gets back inside, drives the car back and forth to.see if it is still in working order, and giggles attend his contribution to our enjoyment of the day. A little later, Zaheer does the same thing again off the same bowler, this time on to the bonnet of an unoccupied car. We are merely shaking our heads in admiration now. He is making batting look far too easy, even on this damp and docile pitch. Just once he attacks as if he were in a fighting rather than a commanding mood. He cover-drives Popplewell for only 2 towards the scoreboard, but he has sprung forward and hit that ball venomously, as though his life depended on striking it away.

At the other end now, the yeoman figure of Shepherd sturdily stands, ready and willing to do his part, but knowing as well as the rest of us that today his will only be a supporting role. He will only score 7 runs in his hour at the crease but even so he stamps character very firmly on this game. It is, I know, fashionable to speak of Shepherd as the bucolic of county cricket, with him minding the family post office down in Devon when the season's done. He lends himself to friendly comments on the nature and gravity of his build by reason of that improbable curve which starts at his ribs and ends in the region of his belt. Will it diminish as the summer wears on? Is there a relationship between it and his run-getting rate? Must the coefficient of July heat be taken into account? The permutations for such speculations are almost endless. It is not only his build, though, that calls the deep-rooted countryman to mind. His bottom hand is clamped massively just above the shoulder of his bat, as some ancestor probably held a scythe, or possibly a black-smith's maul. He stands, ready to back up, with a bunch of knuckles on one hip, head scanning the field of play the way men do by gates when they are contemplating their crops; he almost shades his eyes, even when there is little sun and he is wearing a well-peaked cap. When he runs down the pitch in response to the striker's call, he does so with shoulders squared and arms heavily round, as though he were chivvying bullocks out of a field and into the yard. This isn't the day when he will thump the leather off the ball (it is Zaheer's sixes that cause the umpires to change it halfway through the afternoon), but Shepherd does unloose one cover drive which Hignell somehow manages to intercept. "Well stopped, there!" thunders a gentleman to my left; and so it is. Hignell later catches him with arms stretched high at mid-off and Shepherd comes back puffing slightly from the exertion of that blow. Not much of an innings when set against Procter's or Zaheer's, statistically a failure after what has so far gone before. But Shepherd would have been sorely missed if he had not been at Fenner's today.

When the players emerge from tea, Zaheer needs only two more for his century. As the Cambridge team saunter on to the grass, three girls appear through the gates, dead on cue, and one exchanges medium-range conversation with a fielder, checking up on an evening fixture that she rather more than he seems to have in mind. She suggests six o'clock, with a fine disregard for statutory hours of play, and leads her companions off towards the beer tent on wobbly high heels to begin her long wait. The Cambridge vigil on Zaheer, however, is almost done. A couple of quick singles and he is there, with three 6s and fourteen 4s already making most of his century up. Maybe he had already decided that just 100 would do. The very next ball he is caught behind and, the way he's been playing today, that seems too much of a coincidence to be true. He comes in to as much applause as the small gang of spectators can manage, pats a small boy on the head but is signing no autograph books yet.

Now anti-climax settles upon us all, even though Foat and Graveney can hardly be thought of as the start of the tail. But we have just enjoyed mastery and for them this is not within reach. Each hits a boundary or two, but nobody bothers to applaud these any more. A casual, dreamy spell has fallen upon Fenner's and the blackbirds are beginning to fill the evening with song from the trees around the ground. Gloucestershire are having some batting practice out there and Cambridge are not strong enough to deny them the chance. The bowlers are still being switched and there is much to-do with shifting the double sightscreen opposite the pavilion. Players lean into them at acute angles to the earth, the wheels stick fast and, for a moment, their action is transfixed into an ancient frieze; Egyptians labouring to budge the pyramid stones. The sightscreens roll free, the players detach themselves, the game of cricket goes on. Over in the nets, Shepherd (properly clad) has decided he needs more practice on this unrewarding day. Procter is bowling to him and, good Lord, the man is bowling with his left arm, as though it weren't enough to be the world's finest all-rounder with his right. In the middle, wickets occasionally fall and the bowlers are sticking gallantly to their task. But the day is slipping downhill to its close.

Old gentlemen leave the pavilion and begin to make for home, but are still courteously aware of those who sit by the wall and prefer to stay; they pause, lean on their sticks for a moment before hurrying on, so that they will not obscure our view of a single ball that is bowled. Hignell and Parker race each other in pursuit of one that Brain has certainly hit too far ahead of them to be stopped; but they, double Blues both, are only trying to keep fit. They trot back in tandem, slinging the ball between them as though they were in their Rugby gear. Not much excitement left now; we shall not see Cambridge face the Gloucestershire attack tonight. Brain is still going strong when the last wicket falls, and everyone by then is ready to call it a day. Outside, just across the road, impromptu football is taking place on Parker's Piece. Small boys are reliving the big news of their day, that Cambridge United will go up to Division Two next year. But I am haunted by the memory of P. A. Gibb, who helped to make Procter the cricketer I have just seen.

## GLOUCESTERSHIRE — *First Innings*

| | | |
|---|---|---|
| A. W. STOVOLD c Peck b Gardiner | | 47 |
| A. TAIT c Hignell b Allbrook | | 36 |
| ZAHEER ABBAS c Littlewood b Parker | | 100 |
| M. J. PROCTER c Littlewood b Greig | | 30 |
| D. R. SHEPHERD c Hignell b Popplewell | | 7 |
| J. C. FOAT  b Greig | | 36 |
| D. A. GRAVENEY c Parker b Greig | | 28 |
| J. H. SHACKLETON lbw Howat | | 1 |
| A. J. BRASSINGTON b Howat | | 6 |

B. M. BRAIN not out    23
J. H. CHILDS c Gardiner b Parker    3
    Extras (b 8, lb 8, w 1, nb 3)    20

    Total    337

Fall of wickets: 88, 102, 153, 215, 245, 299, 300, 308, 314.

Bowling: HOWAT 18–6–58–2; GREIG 22–3–73–3; POPPLEWELL 13–3–34–1; ALLBROOK 25–7–71–1; GARDINER 14–4–43–1; PARKER 14.2–3–38–2.

Cambridge University (did not bat): M. K. Fosh, I. G. Peck, P. W. G. Parker, A. J. Hignell, N. C. Crawford, I. A. Greig, N. F. M. Popplewell, S. J. Gardiner, D. J. Littlewood, M. G. Howat, M. E. Allbrook.

Umpires: R. Aspinall and A. G. T. Whitehead.

No further play was possible on the two remaining days because of rain.

# The Roses Match

### YORKSHIRE v LANCASHIRE

ONE APPROACHES THIS DAY AS OTHERS ATTEND A TROOPING of the Colour or a Last Night of the Proms, with a sense of occasion that only participants in a mythology can feel. I was brought up on three legends that combined to keep the family's blood astir, when it might otherwise have grown sluggish with the passing of the years. One was the Lancashire Landing at Gallipoli, where Grandad actually played. Another was the victory of the Wanderers (Bolton's, you understand) at the first Wembley Final, where Dad claims he was fouled by the policeman's white horse. The third was the Roses Match. Not any particular game between Lancs and Yorks, mind; just the Roses Match. This was different from the other two because it was a legend still being made and, by apostolic succession, its future was still partly in our hands. It was of sacramental significance in our calendar, like Whit Walks and Wakes Week, and even if none of us actually got down to Old Trafford or over the hill to Headingley or Bramall Lane, we never went anywhere else while the game was on. Gardening was the order of the day then, with the living room radio going full blast, and Dad sucking his teeth at the tomato plants whenever Washbrook played and missed. Migration to the south in pursuit of trade put a stop to much of my own attendance at the rite, but it dogs me still, as much as any of Francis Thompson's ghosts. When I manage to get up for the Roses Match, I remember who I am and what it is that I am about: not just a spectator at a cricket match this time, but a man with a responsibility to discharge, so that a legend shall live on into the recollection of his children. It is almost the only event which I allow to justify the wearing of a tie, for it is unthinkable that I should turn up (in the enemy camp most of all) without that dark blue silk sprinkled with the neat red roses of my county.

My handicap is that I have always found it hard to whip up the proper degree of belligerence towards the Yorkshire team; much less towards the Yorkshire crowd. There is none more knowledgeable about the game, or fairer in its judgment of skilful play by a cricketer of whichever side. And here, even more than at Old Trafford I think, the spectators themselves are liable to make any cricket match a memorable one. I remember Headingley in the 1961 Test against Benaud's side, when May and Cowdrey were making very heavy weather of the Australian attack. They were together for an age, scoring only a handful of runs, and I think that (when May was out) it must have been the only time an England captain's dismissal was greeted with cheers by Englishmen, so grateful were we that part of our boredom was done. In came Ted Dexter, the young lion of that year, who at once began to call for sharp singles, which had been neglected for far too long. Cowdrey's bulky figure responded gallantly to each call, but they were clearly costing him a lot of puff. After one mighty charge to the other end, in which he only just made his ground, he overran the crease by yards and stood panting in some distress. A "Hey" of relief went round Headingley as the runout was forestalled. As this died down, a voice pickled in the West Riding boomed out from somewhere near my bench. "Now steady on, Dexter. Yer'll 'ave Cowdrey thin as a bloody rake bi close o' play if yer go on like this!" Professional gag men are paid quite a lot of money for lines like that.

That was on such a day as this one, with a hot sun burning from a cloudless morning sky. After the wettest spring I can remember in a long time, with matches rained off all over the land, the weather has turned perfect for our pilgrimage to Leeds. Girls striding towards the match through the trenchwork of bricked terraces off the Otley Road, have abandoned tights in favour of bare legs. Long before the players appear, the caravan by the grandstand is doing brisk business in white sunhats with the Yorkshire colours in a band above the brim; by lunchtime the Headingley crowd will look like a convention from the smarter bowling greens of the south, taking a day off to watch this alien game in the north. But those hats represent commitment as much as protection from the sun, and the hundreds wearing them roar their encouragement when Hampshire leads his team down the dressing room stairs and the players come bounding out on to the turf. Boycott is nursing a sore thumb and Old is out with a bruised foot, absences which must tilt the scales heavily Lancashire's way, but I do not hear anyone round me complaining at this ill-luck. As Wood and David Lloyd come out to bat, Headingley seems to be preparing itself spiritually for a long day of siege, willing its troops to stick to their task without the anointed chief and his most potent aide. I have no doubt, myself, that Hayes was wise in deciding to bat first. After two or three days of this drying heat, that pitch should be good for plenty of runs. No one on the ground can have an inkling of the sensations to come.

Stevenson opens from the Kirkstall Lane end in dead silence and Wood deflects a leg-bye off that first ball. David Lloyd takes guard, plays hastily at the second, and Bairstow is jumping in exultation with the ball gleaming in his palm. The roar that acclaims his catch would not have been greater on the other side of the grandstand in winter, if Leeds had scored a match-winning try against Wigan in the Rugby League. Pilling goes leg before to the third ball of the match and, with Stevenson on a hat trick, Headingley is beside itself with lust. The second roar transcends the first. It is like a thunderclap. Clive Lloyd is almost at the wicket and still the benches and tip-up seats are a-babble with excited reconstructions of just how Yorkshire have made this astonishing breach in Lancashire's walls at their very first assault. We of the Red Rose are taking comfort from the way the great West Indian has come out to bat. He emerges from the dressing room with bat under his arm, still slowly pulling on a glove. The whole of his tall body is relaxed, as though he had just come from a siesta to awaken properly in the sun. His head and shoulders slouch rhythmically with each step he takes and his steps are long, but they are not strides. If a man's walk can be described as a prowl, then Clive Lloyd is prowling to the middle. I think he is the most languid sportsman I have ever seen—but only between balls, whether he is batting or in the field. The big predatory cats move as Clive Lloyd does then, when they are replete and merely wandering between their kills; lazily, supple, with muscle slipping easily over the framework of the bone. He shows not the slightest energy until he reaches the crease where, having taken guard, he steps aside and flexes his knees rapidly, to loosen any stiffness left by those operations last year. The crowd becomes impatient. "Oh come on, Lloyd," some shout. And he does. He strikes that fourth delivery of the first over a casual blow, with a bat which he uses as lightly as a fly swat. A bowler on a hat trick was never more deftly put in his place. You can hear the wind going out of Yorkshire's lungs all round Headingley at that moment.

For the next hour we are treated to batsmanship of brilliance, as Lloyd hooks and drives and clips the bowlers to the boundaries time after time. He does this without the appearance of any effort; every stroke he makes is consistent with the natural looseness of this tall, articulated man. It is as if Stevenson and Cooper were in collusion with Lloyd, serving him with prearranged deliveries so that he can exhibit confidently every aspect of the batsman's art. They are doing no such thing; they are working fiercely to get him out with every ball, but Lloyd is playing everything he gets easily, even when they occasionally find the edge. This is a careless innings, in the purest, not the accepted sense of the word. He hooks at Cooper and the ball flies over the slips for 4. He cuts at Stevenson, fractionally misjudges his stroke again, and puts the ball just short of a fielder off the bottom edge. A good batsman in any game, let alone the Roses Match, would spend the rest of the over, after either of those strokes, watchfully composing himself, thankful that he was not already out. But this is Clive Lloyd and mental retreat is not for him. He accepts his luck without even a shrug and punishes

37

the next ball he receives as though it were the bowler and not himself who had made the mistake. Within three-quarters of an hour Lancashire have 53 runs on the board and Lloyd's share is 41. He hits half a century of his own off only thirty-four balls and eleven of these have gone to the boundary, one of them for 6. For any contest between Lancs and Yorks this is indecent haste: in the first Roses Match I ever saw, Winston Place took four and a half hours to reach his century, Phil King only a little less to hit 120-odd – and that was thought pretty palpitating stuff. For a game beginning as this one did, Lloyd's batting is nothing less than a heresy, as truculent as Luther's at the Wittenberg church door. Most remarkable of all to anyone who only half understands the spirit of a Roses Match, no one at Headingley seems to be minding in the least. This crowd is worthy of Lloyd's display, applauding his boundaries almost as warmly as if he were one of their own. But their loyalties are merely pent-up, to be released in another roar when they think he has been caught in the slips. That was a bump-ball, though; and Lloyd holds up a friendly hand to still the crowd's bedlam and to convey his own feelings of respect.

His going is tragedy for the Red Rose. Wood, who has played acolyte to the great man so far, tries a single off Cope on his own meagre account. He calls for the run and, when Lloyd's knees were unscarred, the West Indian might just have made his ground. But his running is not so swift these days and Stevenson from mid-on has flung the ball to Bairstow, who has the bails off with something to spare. "Keep going, Lloyd," shouts a Yorkshireman in my ear, dispassionate regard for art instantly transformed into partisan zeal. "Well done, Wood," bawls another in withering scorn, which is what Headingley saves for Yorkshiremen who turn out for Lancs. With only one more run added, the renegade from Ossett gets his come-uppance in full and another triumphant roar announces Bairstow's catch behind.

At 79 for four, Lancashire are in trouble again and if Frank Hayes ever needed to show himself at his best, this is the moment to play himself into the England team. He starts well enough and hooks Cooper handsomely for 6, but this morning's plunder of wickets is to be taken mostly at the other end. Stevenson has returned after that solitary over by Cope, and Hughes is despatched while his captain is still getting the feel of the ball. Confronted with Stevenson himself, Hayes now hooks at another delivery that rises head-high, and half the crowd turn towards the dressing room, which is where the ball will surely land. But the fieldsmen are facing the sky above, two or three of them are beginning to run, and Bairstow is streaking like a whippet (pads and all) towards point, leaving the rest behind. He stops, head right back, gloved hands upraised, teeters a step or two forward, three steps to the side, as though staggering under a caber's weight before heaving it away, clasps the ball as it comes to earth behind him, and in doing so falls flat on his back. He has now had a hand in four dismissals, done all that could have been asked; but that one was the best part of twenty yards beyond the line of duty.

Only Stevenson retires from this assault with greater honour and to even more acclaim. There is nothing about his bowling action that will, in itself, make men glad they were here today. He does not flow up to the crease with the smooth menace of Roberts, nor is his delivery the athletic marvel of Thomson, whose body at that moment revolves like a catherine wheel. Stevenson's sturdy figure comes up to bowl like a bull charging a matador's cape, and he hurls them down with something of Fred Trueman's brutish force. Grace and beauty are not in his stars but, today at any rate, his mastery of the bowler's more important objectives is complete. It is his bowling with spirit on length and line that is doing the damage to Lancashire and, after Clive Lloyd's going, no one but Simmons (another sturdy warrior) seems equipped to handle his nagging pace. The others come and go in procession, scarcely adjusted to the brilliant light before they are out again, each fallen wicket hailed by the baying of the crowd. A bunch of Lancashire youths on the terraces are roused to some banal counter-chant, more familiar to the footballer's than the cricketer's ear. "Oh, shut up, you silly Manchester United supporters," mutters a woman, irritated by their unoriginal noise. "Missionaries never got that far," someone suggests, offering an old trans-Pennine thrust. For once, I'm inclined to agree. There is nothing a Lancastrian can decently do at 12.47, with all our wickets gone for a paltry 123, but hold his tongue and acknowledge the hero of the morning's play. We all stand up to clap Stevenson in after the best bowling performance of his career, and even the thrifty Yorkshire committee is moved to mark its approval of 8 for 65 in the Roses Match. Stevenson first played for his county in 1973, but only today does he receive that precious Yorkshire cap.

The Yorkshire innings starts almost as dramatically as ours. While the West Indian Croft is measuring out the thirty-six paces of his run, boos and catcalls break out from some parts of the crowd. Yesterday, at Lord's, one of his bouncers sent Gould to hospital with a badly concussed head and Headingley is threatening him with some form of retribution if he should do the same thing here. Unnerved by this hostility before he has even bowled, Croft presents Yorkshire with 4 byes and a no-ball in his first over, and the catcalls swell mockingly. Then they give way to groans of dismay. For at the other end Hogg removes Athey and Lumb in his first six balls, both of them caught fending off deliveries that have reared viciously from perfectly good length. There is much more in this wicket than first met the eye; all morning, balls have been reaching the batsmen at variable height and, after lunch, Love will be snookered by one that simply shoots straight along the ground. Variable, too, is Headingley's reaction to the fast bowling out there. Hogg looks much more dangerous than Croft because he is forcing the batsmen to play at every ball, but the crowd is accepting his aggressions with nothing louder than the concerted suction of several thousand indrawn breaths. The West Indian is much wilder, therefore more innocuous, but when he does manage to hold his line he is causing the batsmen to duck and weave merely by virtue of his extraordinary height. He must be quite six and a half feet tall, and the final snap-down of his wrist from that altitude makes even the good-length ball rise like a rocket unless it is put into some other orbit by the strangeness of the pitch. Anathema, though, falls on bowler alone. "Play the white man, Croft!" is the wretched cry now, though it comes from someone who earlier was in humour with black Clive Lloyd's most vicious blows. By the long-off boundary, some people are venting their anger on the nearest member of the Lancashire team and Bob Ratcliffe, not a robust man, turns on them unhappily with "Don't tell me, tell him!"

Croft hasn't yet bowled a short-pitched ball, but one of his deliveries has almost parted Love's great shock of hair and the batsman at once signals the dressing room for something to put on his head. By the end of the next over, Headingley is staging a spectacle I had hoped never to see on a cricket ground. Love is wearing reinforced headgear shaped like a jockey's high-crowned cap, but this has a transparent visor that seems to cover the whole of his face. At the other end, Hampshire appears to have borrowed a plain white crash helmet from some friendly motor-cycle cop. The Roses Match has suddenly been translated from an epic struggle of great lineage into something that never was before, with the heirs of Hirst and Rhodes and Leyland now appearing as pantomime figures in some lunar mockery of the game. The bitter taste this leaves is, indeed, partly caused by my feeling that the aesthetic of cricket has been betrayed, but that is only one of several complicated responses.

This resort to armouring the head seems also to be an abdication of the courage which batsmanship in cricket has always required. If first-class cricketers have never realised it before, they should know that the rest of us have hailed them as heroes because their bravery as much as their skill and their grace has far surpassed our own. Even if it does no structural damage, a cricket ball bowled fast inflicts such pain and nausea when it hits the unprotected body that no man will wish it upon himself a second time. The new fashion of helmets is, of course, no more than a logical progression in using protective

devices of one sort or another. Leg guards were introduced in 1800, gloves a little later. No one but a fool
would dream of batting without a metal or a plastic shield
over his genitals, and the past generation has seen the
development of bits and pieces of padding all over the
anatomy. These, being covered by flannels and shirt,
have not offended the aesthete's eye and, so far as I
know, have never caused a murmur of complaint. It is,
therefore, unreasonable of me to be soured by the introduction of something which is as customary in American
football as pads and gloves have been for generations in
cricket. And yet I am, because the most heroic figure of all
is the batsman who will unflinchingly face a bouncer in a
cloth cap or with a bare head and hook the ball to the
boundary, knowing as he begins the stroke that, if he
misses the ball, he will be struck sickeningly, maybe
fatally, upon the skull. No other game employing a ball
demands such downright calculated courage as this. I am
aware that the emotion it arouses does not separate me by
much from the spectator at a bull-fight; I do not like that
thought, but I'm afraid the emotion is there.

I dislike the sight of these helmets and I am sorry to see
cricketers taking refuge in what their predecessors dis-
dained. Yet neither the offensive appearance nor the
nervous spirit are half as deplorable as the circumstances
that have brought these ugly contraptions into the game.
The plain fact is that the bowling of bouncers in the past
few seasons has stained the essentially fair nature of
cricket; and once cricket repudiates the concept of fair
play which it shares with no other game, and which the
Victorians bequeathed, it will be reduced to the shabby
morality of winner takes all. We have Dennis Lillee's
word for it in cold print that he sets out to hurt any batsman whose wicket does not fall quickly, in order to intimi-
date him from the crease; which seems only a semantic
point away from saying that he will remove a batsman by
fair means or foul. Lillee is unique only in that he has
openly admitted what a number of fast bowlers throughout the world now regularly attempt, and I can see no
possible justification for playing cricket in this way. It is

becoming almost daily more remarkable that no first-class cricketer has been killed since Summers of Nottingham-shire was hit between the eyes by Platts of MCC at Lord's in 1870; and it is astonishing that, since Chatfield nearly died at the wicket after being struck by Lever's bouncer at Auckland in 1975, the Laws have not been amended and rigorously enforced.

I do not plead for the elimination of the bouncer altogether, for that alone would not remove potential danger to a batsman, which is inherent in the nature of fast bowling itself. Nor do I think it would be just to remove the bouncer from the bowler's stock in trade when he is confronted with a good batsman in command-ing form. In English cricket such a batsman would be one whose previous seasonal average was, let us say, at least 30 runs in twenty or more innings (which would include fifty-nine county cricketers playing this year). But the ration of bouncers bowled at anybody should be drasti-cally reduced from what has become the habit of today, the bowler being confined by the clear distinction which lies between the occasionally disconcerting and the per-petually intimidating; a dozen bouncers from any fast bowler throughout a team's whole innings would be more than enough. I do not believe it would be contrary to the heroic spirit of the game to forbid absolutely the bowling of short-pitched balls and beamers in any other circum-stances. Ray Lindwall once said that, if he had been unable to get rid of a number nine batsman in a Test match without bowling him a bouncer, he wouldn't have thought himself fit to play for Australia. There is many a fast bowler treading the English cricket grounds this season who, in this sense, isn't fit to be wearing his county cap.

I am, therefore, not as heartened as I should be when Yorkshire go into lunch with 1 run and 9 extras for 2 wickets and two helmets. Better and worse is to follow after the break. In the second delivery of the afternoon, that shooter from Croft disposes of Love, who kicks his leg stump out of its hole in pique and leaves his helmet at the crease to oblige the incoming Sharp; a combination of gestures which, in language worthy of both, seems to say a great deal about where cricket is at. Sharp's occupation of the helmet is little longer than Love's before he, too, is sent back whence he came. More significantly, his head-gear doesn't seem to have done his confidence much good, for he is warding off another flyer from Hogg with his bat when he puts a catch into the slips. If the man had to wear a helmet it would have been tactically much safer, and perhaps more appropriate, if he had headed the ball away in the general direction of silly mid-on. Bairstow comes in with a proper Yorkshire cap on his head and proceeds to stop all manner of rot, gamely striking Hogg to the boundary and Croft for a hectic 3 before, driving at Croft once again, he goes to another catch in the slips.

At 59 for 5, Yorkshire are in even greater trouble than Lancashire were with half their wickets gone – but they have already dropped anchor in the person of their captain for the day. Hampshire was almost out before he had even scored, when he turned a ball from Hogg into the softness of Hughes's forearm and saw it fall to the ground before the fielder could recover from the blow. (Will short leg one day, I wonder, be gauntleted and gloved in iron as the men at arms were who fought for Lancaster and York?) This was to be the turning point in Yorkshire's innings this afternoon. In uncertain singles at first, then with more confident strokes, Hampshire begins to compile a score that will secure his side from being dragged off in the strong current running Lancashire's way. And, for the first time, this Roses Match settles into a tempo more familiar to the connoisseur. By the middle of the afternoon, bowlers and batsmen alike are grafting for their successes in the throbbing heat. The five dismissed batsmen, and the four yet to come, are sunbathing on the deck of the dressing room, outside that glass door which Ian Chappell nearly shattered with his bad temper in the Test of 1975. Some people, who have been on the edge of their benches so far, now take up a nodding acquaintance with the Roses Match as they stroll round the ground in search of ice creams, Ladbroke's odds, anything at all to restore the circulation in their patient limbs. At the Kirkstall Lane end, two members of the ground staff manipulate ropes to prevent the strollers from passing behind the bowler's arm and in front of those high-backed pastel seats which are Yorkshire's method of getting a sight-screen to pay its way per match. But most of us stay put, playing our own historically dogged part. "You reckon it's time for Barry Wood?" asks one, taking note of the wilting Croft. "Nay," says his neighbour, "it's not twilight of the gods already."

By the time Wood does come on to bowl, Carrick has put Yorkshire past 100 without another wicket going down and Hampshire is getting close to his own half century. Croft has been having a miserable time with his run-up, is about to go to pieces altogether when he sinks to his knees at the end of his follow-through as Hampshire hits him for 4. He looks as though all his spirit has gone and Hayes gives the disconsolate fellow a rest. It is Hogg who yields the run that puts Hampshire's 50 on the board and the Yorkshireman will not often have played a more important innings than this. He has seen his side into the lead, helmet and all, and he has deserved every bit of the applause he now gets. Minutes later, Ratcliffe has him leg before and a disappointed supporter bellows "Rubbish!" from the long-off fence as he sees the umpire's finger go up at the appeal. "Perfect position to judge," observes a dry realist in the next row – and I shouldn't be at all surprised if he were a Yorkshireman, too.

Now the burden falls on Carrick who, in the whole of last season, scored only 126 championship runs. There could have been few hopes pinned on him when he began to bat with Yorkshire in the most desperate straits, but something indomitable is in Carrick's soul today. Coming in an hour after Hampshire first took guard, he caught up with his captain's score by the time he had reached 32, and in one sweltering over took 14 runs from the bowling of Hogg. Thereafter his scoring rate slackened, but not once did his resolution or his concentration falter, even after being hit on the elbow by a rising ball from Croft. With Hampshire gone he begins to defend, taking runs only from the looser balls, applying himself to the business of building up that lead with painstaking care and all the time in the world. The cricket ceases to be exciting, but from Yorkshire's point of view it becomes mightily effective. By teatime the score stands at 163 for 6 and Carrick's contribution is a priceless 62. The green sports edition of the *Yorkshire Evening Post* begins to circulate the ground, with its 48-point headline reminding us that "Stevenson Rockets Out Lancs"; but Stevenson now is playing the henchman's part, quietly following Carrick's steady plod. I just wish he had felt proud and cocky enough to bat in his brand-new county cap; but he, too, is playing safe with his features obscured by a visored helm. Carrick has worn nothing at all on his head, has taken everything the bowlers have slung at him without turning a hair, and on such a day as this that has been a triumph in itself.

So measured is Carrick's progress in the evening warmth, so empty of sensation are those last couple of hours following tea, that the events of the morning and early afternoon might well have been part of an entirely different cricket match. Stevenson goes after a while and Cope plays an even briefer supporting role, but Carrick is batting in accordance with an ancient Yorkshire oath which ordains that a man with his eye well in shall proceed solemnly – to the conclusion of the day's proceedings if possible – and leave flights of fancy to transients at the other end. This is still apt to mystify those born south of the Don or the Irwell, but it is well understood by almost everyone at Headingley today. Only those loud lads who have missed their way over the hill from the Stretford End are impatient with Carrick's progress; the rest of us, I suspect, are simply thankful that at least one tradition has been maintained today. Even the wicket seems to be behaving itself now and Jack Simmons, in the slips, is contemplating it thoughtfully with an elbow propped on a forearm, a hand spread across his mouth and jaws, as the bowler returns to his mark after sending down yet another ball which has reached the batsman without startling assistance from the pitch. Alongside Simmons, Clive Lloyd is swinging his arms to and fro, still careless of any fates which may have settled the outcome of the first day's play. Frank Hayes darts here and there about the field, mettling his men by example for one last heave. But when Carrick reaches his century, Yorkshire are 119 runs ahead and Lancashire are already faced with a rearguard action in their second knock.

As Headingley settles down after standing to give Carrick his due, exuberance bubbles up along the tip-up seats. "It's proof that Nature has resumed her normal course," somebody informs the Kirkstall Lane end at large. "We've won two out of the last three Roses Matches. Water's running downhill again." Lancastrians within earshot manage tight little grins at this; even with two days of play potentially still to come, the assumption is perhaps not so very large. Carrick has decided not to tempt Providence by looking for any more runs tonight, but Cooper is now hooking and pulling Ratcliffe to the boundary to rub his side's superiority firmly in, and by close of play Yorkshire stand at 254 for 8. What with those helmets, that cascade of wickets, that 8 for 65 and that 103 not out, the Roses have never known such an engagement as we have just seen. But in spite of the dramas and the penultimate intoxication of a considerable lead over Lancs, some Yorkshire feet remain firmly attached to the ground. "Tell yer what," says one chap, as we all shuffle out in a pack through the gates, "I reckon Barry Wood's the man of the match so far – getting Lloydy's wicket for us this morning."

## LANCASHIRE—*First Innings*

| | |
|---|---|
| B. WOOD c Bairstow b Stevenson | 18 |
| D. LLOYD c Bairstow b Stevenson | 0 |
| H. PILLING lbw Stevenson | 0 |
| C. H. LLOYD run out | 58 |
| F. C. HAYES c Bairstow b Stevenson | 9 |
| D. P. HUGHES c Bairstow b Stevenson | 0 |
| J. SIMMONS not out | 24 |
| J. LYON c Bairstow b Cooper | 5 |

47

| | |
|---|---:|
| R. M. RATCLIFFE c Cooper b Stevenson | 0 |
| C. E. H. CROFT b Stevenson | 4 |
| W. HOGG b Stevenson | 0 |
| Extras (lb 3, nb 2) | 5 |

| | |
|---|---:|
| Total | 123 |

Fall of wickets: 1, 1, 78, 79, 87, 91, 100, 101, 113.
Bowling: STEVENSON 12.1–1–65–8; COOPER 12–3–37–1; OLDHAM 2–0–16–0; COPE 1–1–0–0.

## Second Innings

| | |
|---|---:|
| B. WOOD c Hampshire b Cooper | 22 |
| D. LLOYD c Bairstow b Oldham | 6 |
| H. PILLING lbw Oldham | 7 |
| C. H. LLOYD c Stevenson b Cooper | 16 |
| F. C. HAYES c Bairstow b Cooper | 0 |
| D. P. HUGHES c Love b Oldham | 1 |
| J. SIMMONS c Stevenson b Cooper | 0 |
| J. LYON c Cooper b Oldham | 4 |
| R. M. RATCLIFFE c Bairstow b Cooper | 40 |
| C. E. H. CROFT not out | 0 |
| W. HOGG b Cooper | 0 |
| Extras (b 4, lb 1, w 1, nb 3) | 9 |

| | |
|---|---:|
| Total | 105 |

Fall of wickets: 12, 55, 57, 60, 60, 60, 60, 99, 105.
Bowling: STEVENSON 15–4–42–0; OLDHAM 14–5–28–4; COOPER 9.5–4–26–6.

## YORKSHIRE—*First Innings*

| | |
|---|---:|
| R. G. LUMB c Lyon b Hogg | 0 |
| C. W. J. ATHEY c Hughes b Hogg | 0 |
| J. D. LOVE b Croft | 1 |
| J. H. HAMPSHIRE lbw Ratcliffe | 54 |

| | |
|---|---|
| K. SHARP c D. Lloyd b Hogg | 3 |
| D. L. BAIRSTOW c C. H. Lloyd b Croft | 11 |
| P. CARRICK c Lyon b Croft | 105 |
| G. B. STEVENSON c Lyon b Hogg | 20 |
| G. A. COPE c Croft b Wood | 6 |
| H. P. COOPER not out | 27 |
| S. OLDHAM b Croft | 0 |
| Extras (b 8, lb 3, w 1, nb 21) | 33 |
| | |
| Total | 260 |

Fall of wickets: 6, 7, 10, 20, 59, 137, 176, 195, 256.

Bowling: CROFT 20.5–5–58–4; HOGG 21–4–73–4; RATCLIFFE 16–2–59–1; WOOD 9–4–18–1; HUGHES 2–0–16–0; SIMMONS 4–3–3–0.

Umpires: D. L. Evans and W. E. Phillipson.

Yorkshire (19 pts) beat Lancashire (4 pts) by an innings and 32 runs on the second day.

# The County Championship

FOR MORE THAN A HUNDRED YEARS, FIRST-CLASS CRICKET IN England has been founded upon competition for the county championship, and this is still the contest that ranks above all the rest. I imagine there are people who can recite the list of county champions since 1864, while being uncertain who won which of the other trophies that various sponsors have offered in the past fifteen years. Grudgingly or gracefully, they have had to accept the fact that the county championship might now be extinct if the one-day events hadn't drummed up a new army of recruits to the watching of the game, and if commerce hadn't been persuaded to circulate some of its spare cash around the county grounds in exchange for freely advertising its goods: non-smokers can no longer afford to abhor the names of John Player or Benson and Hedges, the bearded must not disdain the attentions of Gillette and, since last season began, the man who likes his liquor neat should not look blearily upon the image of Schweppes. All the same, the johnny-come-latelies must not expect the rest of us to yield too much of our affections simply because social and economic history has at last caught us cap in hand. The county championship, after all, speaks of something more than cricket, as the briefer county contests do only by extension. This is where deep tribal loyalties of the English have been cherished for generations in the most civilised fashion possible. It is not only Lancastrians and Yorkshiremen who are sentimental about the counties of their birth, whose names and

50

individual characters were forged long ago in the making of this land. I do not think that the grey men who revised our boundaries a few years back, concocting new names and abolishing old ones for their convenience alone, could have felt either cricket or English history in the marrow of their bones. One day my grandchildren, yet unborn, will probably wonder what and where Rutland was; and I would like to think that, if Rutland had ever raised a county championship team, this might not have been so, in spite of its obliteration from government's map.

There will not be a body at the County Ground this Saturday morning who does not feel such loyalty tugging from his roots. Neither Northants nor Worcester can have any hope of taking the championship this year unless there is some monumental disturbance of form from one end of the table to the other; with a quarter of the fixtures already played, both are among the bottom four teams. So when Cook wins the toss and decides to bat first, we can be sure that the two or three hundred spectators are here for cricket and ancestral honour alone, and not for the thrill of camp-following a successful side. They are not expecting rapid drama, either, although cricket can provide that at any old hour. To a man and a woman they are faithful followers of the championship match which, played over the course of three days, has been both the nursery and the consummation of the game. I don't think there's any doubt that limited-overs cricket has improved the quality of fielding in this country almost out of recognition, and for that many thanks indeed; otherwise it has subtracted from the infinite variety of skills which cricket evolved and refined in the three-day championship match, and the virtual disappearance of the leg-spinner is but the most notorious example of this loss. As Vanburn Holder's bow legs gallop to the crease for the first over, an elderly woman passing the West Stand hails a contemporary already in his place. "How are you?" she asks. "Oh, not too bad, Mrs Lyman," he replies, flashing the single peg left in his upper jaw. "One year older"; and he grins again. Perhaps the pair of them have enough time, these days, to watch a championship match from first ball to last, with its thoughtful passages as well as its dramatic bursts in the maturing strategies of attack and counter-attack. And if they don't, this day alone will show enough of technique and grace and character to feed memory and devotion for the remainder of their lives.

There is a fiction that championship matches start at snail's pace because the players feel they have so much time in hand, but Cook and Larkins are soon giving the lie to that. Almost a run a minute comes in the first half hour as those two men in maroon caps seek to assert them-selves against the Worcestershire attack. Cook, having edged a boundary to get off the mark, is the more careful of the two, but Larkins is unbridled from the first ball he receives. He plays and misses Pridgeon once or twice but is not put off by this and turns the bowler off his legs for 4, then square cuts Holder beautifully to the fence. Within the hour the batsmen are up with the clock and the West Stand sages affirm that this is quite a reasonable start, as Norman Gifford rearranges his bowling to take the first ascendancy away from Northants. Holder gives way to Cumbes, and Pridgeon changes ends. He now bowls with an arc of cars behind him and, beyond them, an expanse of coarse and balding grass which is half the playing area of Northampton Town, an impecunious club whose dilapidated stand crouches along the length of the distant touch-line. The pause for this rearrangement allows the spectators to speculate upon the weather, which could take a hand in this cricket match before it is done. Some-one recalls that the long-range forecasters promised us unusual warmth to the middle of June, and here we have yet another dull and chilly day. But people are still saun-tering into the ground with their haversacks and their shopping bags laden with thermos and sandwiches; and, between each over, one or two more cars glide round the boundary to join those already behind Pridgeon. I think it is perhaps the spectators more than the players who give championship cricket a leisurely name.

Cumbes labours for a while from the pavilion end, but in the twenty-fourth over Holder is brought back and the first drama of the match occurs. The West Indian's third ball flies off the edge of Larkins's bat straight to the cupped hands of Turner at slip – and falls to the ground. Holder's hands go to his hips in frustration but his shoulders are resigned. He glares only for an instant at the fieldsman who, at that moment, is emotionally isolated from his team-mates by the size of his error. A difficult catch missed would have got a sympathetic word from the keeper or someone else as close. This one causes the others to look at the floor or up at the sky, anywhere except at Turner, who is rubbing his hands where the ball stung. Then he reaches for his handkerchief and blows his nose in the oppressive silence hanging over the infield. A few minutes later, the Worcestershire spirits rise again when Cook, impatient with his own cautious rate, swings at Pridgeon and is caught by Humphries behind.

"It'll slow up now," says someone, cocking his eye at the scoreboard's 79 for 1, as Steele's bare head bobs down the pavilion steps. "Come on, David," murmurs a less mournful voice, hoping that England's hero of three seasons ago will today emerge from the doldrums of this year. Steele may have been going through a bad patch of late (though he got a few against Essex, someone recalls) but there is still something in his approach to the wicket that would hearten any team in need of runs. It is the bustling walk of the tradesman on whose service you can always rely, and that untimely grey hair above the spectacles only makes Steele look the most dependable tradesman in town. He taps the ground with his bat as he comes eagerly towards the game, and when he is in it, and backing up at the bowler's end, he crouches a little, alert and ready to dash forward with whatever the customers may need. Thus he watches Larkins defend for a few balls, practising his own strokes on the side each time the bowler returns; when his own moment comes, he tries to get Holder away to leg several times, but mostly he is going forward to stifle the ball. Then he dabs at one outside the off-stump, pulling his bottom hand away at almost the same time, knowing (with a sudden spurt of sweat, no doubt) that he has been lucky to touch that ball past the wicketkeeper for 4. A couple of singles come his way, both of them deflected with the same unease. Then Steele dabs at another delivery that on another day he might have struck soundly off the back foot wide of gully's right hand, but which today he would have done well to leave alone with shouldered arms. This time the dab flicks the ball to Hemsley, who takes it at the second attempt low down in the slips. David Steele has not been in long enough to put his game together again and only a couple of claps are heard as he returns to the pavilion as eagerly, it seems, as when he emerged.

In the West Stand an old chap who has been keeping careful score sighs heavily, closes his book and begins to move off. "Coming back this afternoon?" asks a crony nearby.

"No," he says, "umpiring this afternoon over at Dallington."

"Oh-ho," rumbles the other, "better be careful, then"; and, as the one strolls away round the track, the other opens a battered attaché case, brings out pork pie, some salad, knife, fork and proper pot plate, arranges the lot on the closed case across his knees, and begins to take an early lunch.

Larkins has prospered all this time, however, and with his own score, Northamptonshire's has steadily grown. When the cricketers go in to lunch, the two fallen wickets have been exchanged for 122 runs and Larkins stands at 70 not out. The crowd has every reason to be pleased with such a well-founded start and the youngsters are shrill with enthusiasm as they play their own knockabout cricket by the boundary placards advertising this and that. ("Is it 4," one enquires, settling the ground rules before they begin, "if it goes past the Burnley Building Society?") Lunch over, Larkins moves on, the tiny figure of Williams at the other end strives, and Gifford again manipulates his bowling to maintain any distraction that the meal break may have begun. He puts himself on at the pavilion end and appeals loudly for lbw against Williams at his very first ball. "'E's at it again," observes a Northants supporter, who has seen the Worcester captain at work many times before. The ploy doesn't succeed at once, but the general strategy does when Williams, goaded into doing something by Gifford's twirling spin, and his supplication to the gods when the umpires are unmoved, sweeps, misses, and gets his leg in the way of the ball. Larkins has reached 92, and since being missed by Turner he has done nothing dangerously wrong. Almost every over has added to his score and the longer he is there the more commanding he looks. But now a strange pause interrupts his progress towards the century. It takes him one hour and five minutes to move from 92 to 99 and impatience begins to rustle round the County Ground. There is no slow hand-clapping, for Wayne Larkins of Bedfordshire belongs to Northants; he is being given the benefit of all East Midlands doubts, but the impulse to jeer is evidently there. This is misplaced, for the central drama of cricket is emphasised in Larkins's present plight.

This game is at all times a gladiatorial contest between two players, a batsman and a bowler, and everyone else taking part in a match is, at the moment of conflict between those two, playing no more than an auxiliary role. The batsman has his partner, who relieves his isolation with some moral support, but is essentially there for the purely statistical purpose of registering a valid run. The bowler has ten aides in the field, but they are helpless to act until that swift cut and thrust, that intensely private moment between batsman and bowler, is done. This numerical advantage of players to the bowling side, however, creates a situation which is almost unique to cricket. It makes batting, consequently the scoring of runs, an act of defiance by one man against a vastly superior force who control the ball at all times, except in that split second when it touches the bat. Among team games played with a ball, this is also true of baseball alone; but no other sport knows such an heroic stance.

From the boundary today it is hard to see any difference in the playing of the pitch between 2.45 and 3.50. The bowling of Gifford and Patel, Holder, Pridgeon and Cumbes, appears to be no more tantalising, no more hostile, when Larkins is clearly struggling to defend his wicket than when he was clumping the bowlers aggressively to the ropes. While he is making those seven agonised runs, Willey comes out, knocks up a useful 24 and departs again, and Yardley settles down to some ebullient strokes. The sun begins to beam upon the ground but Larkins stays in the dimness of his own obscuring light. The nervous nineties surely never plagued anyone more than this, and the defiance of a batsman was never more tortured to behold. From a cavalier charge as Rupert of the Rhine, poor Larkins has suddenly been translated into Horatius at the Bridge, and the Etruscans of Worcestershire are hemming him in. The spectators think him a dull dog now but out there, in the middle, it is wits against determination, anxious anticipation meeting the premeditated blow. Gifford, turning at the end of his short run, rolls up his eyes to his aide at mid-on; it is a signal to be ready for a response the bowler will now try to extract from the batsman with this one finely calculated ball. At the striker's end Larkins crouches, not yet knowing the degree of spin Gifford is about to apply, or the trajectory of the missile through the air, or just where on the stubbled turf the ball will pitch. The ball is unloosed by the crafty hand and in the quickness of its flight the batsman summons his eye, his technique, his knowledge and his strength into one co-ordinated movement of his own. As Gifford's delivery pitches fractionally short in a temptingly fulsome arc and turns towards the leg-stump in its upward bounce, Larkins steps forward, left elbow high, bat utterly straight, only the toe of his back foot remaining where he stood, and brings the blade down like a scythe at a precise angle which sends the ball gently along the ground to where mid-on was waiting for a catch. Once more the attackers are defied, in another instant the gladiators will clash again. Larkins straightens up, removes his cap, wipes the moisture of strain as much as warmth off his brow. So the duel between batsman and bowler, the drama of cricket, goes on.

Then suddenly he strikes Holder away for two runs, at 3.56, and he has his century at last. A natty

Citroën and a red MG detach themselves from the ring of vehicles at the football end and slip away round the boundary while Larkins is raising his bat at the applause. The drivers are probably content to have seen him reach three figures, but they will miss the best of Larkins today. Having painfully struggled through those last few runs to his hundred he now becomes a different man, even more cavalier than when he plundered the bowling up to 92. He has passed through a psychological barrier, and it is comparable to the effect on track athletes after Bannister ran the first four-minute mile. Citroën and MG are scarcely out of sight before Larkins has belted Pridgeon over the boundary at long-on, where the outfielder eventually has to lie full length to recover the ball from under the Northamptonshire President's car. After tea, Larkins takes the Worcestershire bowlers one by one, and pays them back crushingly for the confinement they had earlier imposed. In just fifteen minutes straddling five o'clock, he hits 35 runs as he rushes from 125 to 160. The sunshine now floods the ground, so that the cricketers are dazzlingly white upon the vivid green of the grass, with that solitary maroon cap glowing warmly in its own pool of brilliant light. A couple of hundred people have spent most of their day so far watching the game behind windscreens, but many of them emerge now to enjoy the bright swing of his bat as it cracks the ball this way and that. Yardley is having his fun, too, and Northants are feeling very well when the 300 goes up with three overs left before their innings must close. As almost every local knows, Larkins is approaching the highest score of his life, the 167 he got against Warwickshire a couple of seasons ago. Will he better it now, with only eighteen more balls to be bowled and Yardley glad to be among the runs on his own account? The bowlers are tiring after nearly five hours of work, the outfielders beginning to pant a little from their perpetual chasing since tea. Norman Gifford's pink face looks as if it might be about to boil over from some combustion within. But Worcester are not going to present Larkins with his record on a plate and they have him fidgeting again as he goes for those last few runs. He gets them, though, and when Northants go in at 312 for 4 he is still unbeaten with 170 in the book. It's been a fine innings, with much light and some shade, and I can see why there is talk that he might play for England one day, for there was great character in that score as well as lovely strokes.

Thus Act One finishes, with the likelihood that Northants have already put themselves beyond danger of defeat. Cricket matches, however, are not always settled by the struggles of mortal men alone, and in the course of three days the weather is quite capable of turning certainties, let alone likelihoods, upside down. But Worcestershire's first task must be to build a first innings score close enough to that of Northants to secure themselves at least a draw: the initiative is with the home side and the visitors must wrest it away.

From the outset, Northants set a field to take close catches and be hanged to the incidental loss of a boundary or two; get a couple of wickets tonight and Monday morning will be promising indeed. At third slip Larkins is euphoric, windmilling his arms, chattering non-stop, too excited by his score to keep still or quiet except when it matters, when the ball is being bowled; but then, I imagine, his moustache bristles up at the memory of his fight. Turner must have that somewhere on his mind, too, for the catch he dropped cost Worcestershire nearly 130 runs. He stands at the crease like a slender Regency buck, with his shirt collar upturned so that his chin and his mouth are tucked out of sight inside its sharp points. A neat and stylish batsman, who has been one of the best in the world, and New Zealand cannot be happy that he has decided not to tour England with them in his Worcestershire benefit year. This is the wicket Northants would like to have most of all before close of play and in the first half hour of Turner's innings they twice show that they are terribly keen. First Griffiths, then Lamb, raps him on the pads. Both times there is a strident chorus of appeal and Turner is surrounded by infielders with arms and legs splayed in mid-air, like a war party of Maoris in the last convulsion of a haka before they go for his pakeha blood.

Having seen such sights since birth, he is unmoved and steadily forges ahead, hooking Griffiths magnificently for 4 immediately after the first appeal. At the other end the dark and sleek Ormrod, more solid and with less whip-cord in his build, thumps singles off the ball and gives the bowlers no change. As the clock on the pavilion moves towards half past six, Northamptonshire's evening ambi-tions gently die. When the players come in and their long shadows waver into one great dark beam as they merge across the grass, Worcester are 54 runs to the good, with Turner on 33 and Ormrod on 17.

Time was when county professionals put their feet up on a Sunday (though the gentlemanly players might be found out at golf) but that all ended when the John Player League came in and the Lord's Day Observance Society began to go out. This weekend see these two sides in a one-day tussle over at Milton Keynes, which Worcester-shire win. A certain moral advantage is theirs, then, when the cricketers muster at the County Ground again on Monday morning. Half an hour before plays starts on a dull and almost listless day, Cumbes may be seen lapping the football pitch in his track suit, with "Worcester CCC" in green letters across his back. The rest of the team are finishing their nets by the scoreboard while, on the other side of the field, Griffiths is leading half a dozen lads of the Northants county colts in high catching practice. Between these two groups, the groundsman perched on his orange tractor is mowing the outfield grass and the juice in the clippings sweetens the air with a country smell. The popping exhaust and the grunts and occasional shouts of the cricketers echo in this otherwise empty corner of the town. When Peter Willey, already dressed for play, crosses from the corner shop in the narrow street outside the gates, the sprigs on his boots grate on the stone and can be heard fifty yards away, for there is not another soul in sight. Perhaps twenty-five cars will be drawn up on either side of the sightscreen at the football end when play begins, where on Saturday the traffic was in two rows filling the whole arc. A dozen or so spectators lounge in the pavilion seats which are exclusive to

"Gentlemen members only": it is a small building, not far removed in size or mood from the village green, and a pair of cricket boots with owner attached are propped up on the sill of the Worcester dressing room, a foot or so above a gentlemanly head. A few more figures may be seen elsewhere on the ground and in front of the pavilion sightscreen four boys are batting a tennis ball about. When an old man comes to the pavilion door and shakes a handbell at the world to inform it that play will start in ten minutes sharp, he does not expect this to be a galvanising noise. Championship cricket in Northampton on a Monday morning begins the way Sunday mornings everywhere generally feel, with occasional pensive movements to whatever the Almighty has in mind.

Tranquillity is the best word to use about the morning's play. Turner and Ormrod collect 3 runs from the first over and the New Zealander survives another lbw appeal. A little later, when 25 overs of the innings have been bowled, the umpires and half the Northamptonshire side congregate over the inadequacies of the modern ball, but the umpires decide that Northants must carry on with this one for a while and forget about the good old days when balls were always made by hand and their stitching did not so quickly fray. It is not as though the batsmen have been knocking the thing about; most of their runs are in deflected ones and twos. The openers are by no means in the same toils that Larkins knew on Saturday afternoon. They are getting their runs regularly, each over after over, but they are collecting them unhurriedly, as if they were on the dole. There are thirteen pigeons at the County Ground today and I don't believe their foraging of the outfield between long-on and long-off is once disturbed while Worcestershire potter along in the general direction of lunch. Cook, temporary captain in the absence of Watts, decides that something drastic must be done before we all go back to sleep. He will now try to buy a wicket, Turner's above all, so he brings in his spin and spreads his field wide, placing most of his men in a network to the off. The tactic very nearly succeeds almost as soon as it is begun. Willey gets the New Zealander to sky one so that mid-on only has to wait for it to drop; but poor young Richards then drops it himself and stares wretchedly at the ground. Turner, understanding these things well, continues as placidly as before. Somehow or other – and I almost can't see how – he is piecing together a score that may go on for a century or even longer. Northants are getting through a tidy rate of overs, 19 in the first hour to be followed by 22 in the second, and this is not nearly the most hostile bowling side in the county championship. Yet the batsmen pick only 45 runs from the first hour, merely 41 from the second, which is not the way they generally go about things in Worcestershire when the fruit harvest comes round. The sluggishness of those two men in green caps can only be explained in terms of a strategy for retarding the game and making sure their county goes home with a draw. An arena full of restless watchers would test their nerve to bat in this soporific way, but any man who exhorted them to buck up this morning would embarrass himself conspicuously in the wide open spaces of the County Ground and so the spectating, like the batting, passes the time in muted self-restraint.

Never was lunch more welcome than when Worcestershire have dawdled to 140 runs without loss on a grey day against Northants. The players drift off to their refuelling station beyond the groundsman's shed, where rollers and mowers smell of grass and oil, and an ancient Ewbank mangle stands rustily with faded Axminster at its feet, ready for mopping up when the English monsoon breaks again. In a refreshment hall beside the pavilion, Colin Milburn sips tea and chats with old chums, twinkles cheerfully with his one good eye and makes the plastic chair creak uneasily under his generous weight. Now there's a man who would never have spent such a morning with a bat in his hands. Wistful he must be, but I wonder even more what he makes of the schoolboys by the sightscreen a few yards away. They are at their knockabout with the tennis ball again but this time, heaven help us, one of them has a motor-cyclist's helmet on his head.

Over the eternal salad of the county cricketer's lunch, someone in the Worcestershire camp has directed a change of course. Turner and Ormrod return to the crease as men making up for lost time and within fifteen minutes put another 23 runs on the board. Ormrod then flicks at a rising ball from Lamb and is caught behind. Half an hour after lunch Turner's century arrives and the man actually runs three to get it; a little later he drives Williams straight into the pavilion for 6, being perhaps shamed into such a stroke by Neale, who has just done the same thing off Steele. Now the bowling of Northamptonshire is being put into perspective, as it should have been all along, and in the first hour of the afternoon's play 82 runs are rattled up. Neale has become the pacemaker, carving swathes through the air and brightening the drab day, as Turner and Ormrod in tandem had dulled it even more. Contentment begins to spread among the sprinkle of watchers and, once more, the red brick back yards round the ground echo a little to the spatter of applause. Neale is going to cost Northants a bonus point or two if he goes on like this, as Turner is about to do almost by default, but at least life is restored to the bloodstream of the game.

Suddenly, at twenty-past three, the heart leaps at a glorious piece of cricket. Cook has been playing a very thoughtful part ever since Worcestershire began to bat. He has a side of limited talent and even less experience; six of his men are apprentices to this trade, but they have been warmly encouraged by Cook, who has applauded every decent throw from the boundary to the wicket-keeper, had a word now and then with young bowlers who might be starting to flag. No bowler himself, his example has been confined to the field. His strategy of trying to buy wickets has not really come off and the innocence of those young bowlers has had much to do with that. Only Willey is practised enough to bait Cook's trap with skill and, the one time the bait was taken, the prey managed to get away. At 233 for 1, however, Willey gets another bite when Turner strikes him into the air towards the football end. As the batsman hits that ball, the only doubt in his mind can be whether he has lifted it high enough to carry for 6, or whether it will drop a little short of the boundary and roll over the edge for 4; it is a fine, full-blooded shot destined for runs in the region of long-on, with no fielder nearly within reach. But Cook himself has been lurking deep, almost behind the bowler's arm and, as the bat strikes the ball, he begins to run desperately to his right, trusting his instinct for the ball's swirling path through the air. As it hums to earth just inside the ropes, Cook is still a couple of paces away, but he lengthens that last stride, stretches forward with his right hand, and snatches the ball from the air at the level of his knee. I've seen baseball outfielders do something of the sort, with a leather bucket of a glove on their hands and a final tumble across the grass to emphasise the difficulty of their feat. Cook's hand is bare and, though he staggers a little, he stays upright and merely looks pleased.

With Turner gone, Worcestershire are completely swing and clout, as Neale and Hemsley together head for the last two batting points before the innings must close. One run after these have been secured Neale goes, hitting as he came, scooping the ball round to David Steele at deep square leg, where those capable hands clasp it with a thud alongside the fielder's ear. Another 7 runs and Act Two is done. Worcestershire have achieved their first objective and, with the scores in perfect balance, the match is almost certainly settling into a draw. But then, just after tea, the visitors strike a powerful blow that could lead to a win, as Holder gets Larkins lbw with only 18 runs added to Northamptonshire's scanty lead of 4. If Worcester can also heave Cook and Steele aside at small expense, and if the weather holds for the remaining sessions of play, Northants could be hard pressed to save this game. There is, perhaps, something of rearguard in their approach with their most successful batsman so quickly out; only 40 runs come in the first hour after tea. Gifford, ever optimistic about his own chances of changing the course of a match, brings himself into the attack and, at ten to six, with Northamptonshire no more than 61 runs ahead, he puts them even more firmly with their backs to the wall. Cook tries to sweep from outside the off-stump (a voice in the pavilion declares him an idiot even as he makes the stroke) and, in a swither of dust and capsizing pads, as disordered now as he was magnificently poised when making his catch, misjudges everything and is bowled.

At 57 for 2, Northants could wish that Steele were in much better batting form. His second innings has started in much the same fashion as his first came and went. He has played forward to the first delivery of pace from Holder and, through no management of Steele's, the ball has only just missed the shoulder of the bat. He prods and pushes uncertainly for a while longer. Then Pridgeon manages the nearest thing to a bouncer that this pitch will produce: but the ball comes off its short length too slowly to endanger an old hand like Steele and he slaps it for 4 runs off the fullness of his bat with a smack that makes you wince fifty yards away. This one stroke becomes the turning point in his game. It seems to remind him of three summers ago, when he came from obscurity to Lord's and played Lillee and Thomson like just another pair of fast bowlers he might never have met before, carefully, bravely, with a technique that did not desert him in the general panic at their names: it was self-respect as much as anything that, by the season's end, sent David Steele back to Northampton and a wealth of lamb chops as a national hero who had restored England's cricketing guts. As I say, that boundary off Pridgeon this evening seems to stir Steele's memory of his first innings at Lord's, when thrice he hooked Lillee's bouncers away, where others had been ready to duck before the Australian had even bowled. Gradually his other shots begin to work now off the Worcestershire attack, and you can see the tension slipping out of his body, as he moves into strokes with muscular flow instead of shaping up in nervous spasms and constipated jerks. Some time before play closes, Steele reaches his 50 and holds his bat high in triumph and to salute his admirers in return. Relaxed now, seeing the ball well, he goes on a little longer until Northants are

129 for two, himself at 64, and the Worcester advance has been held at bay.

Grey and greasy clouds are schooning overhead when the last day's play begins, and the umpires look at them anxiously as they walk out to the square. Holder touches his toes to keep warm at the end of his run while Cecil Cook keeps him waiting until the pavilion clock reaches 11 am precisely. At the West Indian's second ball a nearby church chimes the hour, at his fourth Williams takes a single, leaving Steele to play the last two with concentrated ease. Gifford opens from the pavilion end and is cover-driven for 4 off his first delivery by Williams, a small and chubby young man who looks as if he might be sweating rather a lot even in this cutting breeze. He will bat this morning to instructions from above, to hold the fort until enough time has passed to preserve Northants from the possibility of defeat, and then perhaps to try and make some runs. Steele, too, acknowledges local requirements, and in the first hour the pair of them add 49 careful runs, which is just about the tradesman's rate for the job. Shortly after noon, with Northants on 179, Williams goes too far forward to Gifford, senses rather than sees the spin loop over his bat, and gets himself stumped. After that, no one partners Steele for very long. Willey, trying to force the pace, spoons a dolly catch after hitting a couple of 4s and returns to the pavilion gritting his teeth in self-disgust. Yardley stays for a couple of overs and is then despatched. "What a shame," says a motherly soul, carrying a tray of tea over to the scorers in their box, "he's only got 3." Yardley is a man who inspires maternal thoughts, with his jokes, his giddy laughter, his chatterboxing to all around. This seems to be a characteristic of Worcestershire (whence Yardley came to Northants) and today Gifford's men do not appear to have much serious business on their minds. They are forever poking each other in the ribs, giving each other playful pushes, performing stiff-limbed mimes when they have fielded the ball.

Steele, meanwhile, is carrying on a treat. He made his name on the county circuit as a forward player but his most notable stroke this morning is something off the back foot that is liable to put the ball anywhere between the covers and third man, the bat finishing at the high port with his right wrist in front of his mouth. He uses it to reach his century through extra cover to the ropes, and he is balanced on tiptoes, erect, as he watches the ball go. He has, no doubt about it, recaptured his form in this innings, but the wily Gifford has him just before lunch. He changes ends and, in his first over with the football ground behind him, he holds a ball back, Steele forces it too soon and lofts a simple catch to mid-on. The only question now is when Northants will declare and whether there will be anything for Worcester to challenge when they do. A draw, which seemed the likeliest result after the visitors all but came level in their first innings, looks even more probable when Cook lets his men bat on after the break. He can hardly be blamed for his caution, with little more than honest triers in his pace attack. When the declaration comes, just after half past two, Worcestershire need 270 runs to win in 180 minutes left for play and, unless they make an outstandingly aggressive start, this is not a ratio that might tempt the visitors to throw their own caution to the wind.

When Act Four begins, then, we are liable to see the sort of thing that has too often given the county championship a dreary name, with two or three batsmen playing out time against phlegmatic bowling and everyone on the ground simply hanging about till close of play. In fact, the most exciting cricket of the match occupies this Tuesday afternoon. It begins with Turner taking two runs through the covers off Griffiths's first ball. He plays defensively at the second, drives again at the third – and Sharp flings himself horizontally to the right, gloves and pads turning upwards as his body goes through the air, as a shark's body twists when it is going for the kill. Godfrey Evans in his prime never took a better wicketkeeping catch, nor one which more transformed an apathetic day. It gives Northants the spur they need and, for a moment or two, it rouses Worcestershire as well. That over costs their most precious wicket but it also brings 5 runs and, by the time Lamb has bowled his first six balls from the pavilion end, the visitors have 13 on the board. Thereafter, any thoughts they may have had of winning evaporate in perfunctory singles occasionally augmented by 2s. No one bowls a maiden until eight overs have gone down, yet after the eleventh over the score is but 25 for 1, and that is not nearly a victorious rate. There is a curious psychological block in Worcestershire's way, for only one Northamptonshire man stands on the boundary and in a one-day game this would be an invitation to hit out. It is almost as if, this being a match of more exhausting length, their sights are now set on the blackening of the clouds above and the chance that these may release them soon from any further need to work.

Northamptonshire, though, think they see a silver lining at the very moment when Worcestershire must believe the match is certain to be drawn. They have been batting for fifty minutes and they have scored 38 runs with only Turner lost. Ormrod has lately hit 4 off Willey, who has relieved Lamb at the pavilion end. He then aims a blow at Griffiths and, even as he aims it, you can see the indecision in his mind; shall it be a firm defensive stroke in keeping with the tempo of a game that will shortly be drawn, or shall he take advantage of that open field and give himself the purely personal pleasure of another 4? He does neither the one thing nor the other and Griffiths has him lbw. Cook, at this, draws his field even more tightly round the pitch and, in the next over, himself catches Neale off Willey at silly mid-off; and Worcestershire are 42 for 3. There should be a great crowd to share the drama these cricketers are acting now and, if there were, loud roars would rattle those back street windows and reverberate around the dark cavern of the football stand. Instead, a couple of dozen people sit tensely by the pavilion steps, and maybe as many more sit in cars with their windows down, not one of them daring to shout lest they violate some code peculiar to the average weekday on the county cricket grounds. "It might be Dolly's day," one speculates to another, as the next batsman comes down the steps. "'E's 'ad 'is day," the other assures him when D'Oliveira passes within reach. No wonder international cricketers have stayed more modest than other sportsmen, by and large.

D'Oliveira comes on to the field whirling his batting arm to flex muscles that have so far hardly been exercised in this match. He spent ten minutes at the crease in the first innings, has bowled half a dozen overs at Northants; otherwise, he has been a figure of charm rather than activity for two and a half days. He walks out with a certain gravity, partly due to the occasion and partly to his now dignified shape, and those dark brown eyes contain – only for the moment, no doubt – nothing but resolve. Hemsley, awaiting him, is a rugged-looking chap, and if this pair cannot stop Northamptonshire's attack for an hour or so, Worcester might be in a sorry state, for with them the side's batting experience ends. But after only 8 more runs Hemsley goes, playing across the line of Griffiths's pace, which is enough for him to catch the ball as it rebounds off the batsman's pad. This is a strong young bowler, who has been the spearhead of Northants this season while Sarfraz has been touring with Pakistan, and determination is carrying him splendidly along. As he walks away to start his eleventh over, he gives the ball a rub under his armpit and polishes fiercely at the result, then turns and pounds back heavily for more. It is his last fling of the day, though. After seventy-five minutes, Williams replaces him at the football end, so that Worcestershire must deal entirely with spin. For the off-breaks of Willey, Cook now brings up a claustrophobic line of three men along the very edge of the pitch on the leg side, himself threatening the batsman in the middle of the three. Instantly his tactic works and he has taken his second brilliant catch of the game. As Patel drives to shift that trio to safer ground for him and them alike, Cook swivels round to avoid being hit, has his back to the pitch, is almost doubled up; but the corner of his left eye spots something flying past and with astonishing reflex he grabs it with his right hand – and is carried a couple of yards by the velocity of the ball lodged in his palm. That makes Worcester 57 for 5 and Northants can begin to think they might win this match. Only D'Oliveira, surely, can now bar their way.

He is composed; which, to Northants, is the most ominous sign. The disappearances of Hemsley and Patel have only made more purposeful his smothering of almost every ball he has received. He has watched each delivery every centimetre of the way, not taken his eye off it until the ball has lain inert within a yard or two of his feet. Only then has he allowed himself to come upright again, to put his head back and draw a deep breath, now and then to brush some hair over the makings of a luminous pate. Once in a while, having decided that the coast is clear, he indulges in a single, possibly as a relief from all that bending; and, just once, the old tigerish D'Oliveira is unleashed as he cracks Willey for 4 to the deep extra cover boundary. He is batting, mind, with tension thickening by the minute round that wicket; but, even so, humour is allowed to curl in. Dolly comes up grinning from one of his most deliberate defensive strokes, and it is probably Yardley who has just tickled him pink. When Sharp plunges like a ferret to extract a dead ball from between the batsman and his stumps, it is Yardley who pretends to chop him to the ground with a karate blow, and half Northamptonshire as well as Dolly get a giggle out of that. I'm not at all surprised the French have never understood this game, whose players cannot be *sérieux* when their honour is at stake.

When the players come out after tea, D'Oliveira's first thought is to look at the sky, where the clouds are sagging thickly with gloom and damp. If Northants claim the extra half hour, as they surely will, he and the Worcestershire tail must hang on for seventy minutes now to avoid defeat; but perhaps those clouds will help. For twenty minutes before the break, the old soldier has managed to keep Humphries out of harm's way most of the time by getting a single of each over's final balls. With every Northamptonshire player except the bowler now crouched within a few yards of the bat, D'Oliveira succeeds in keeping the first three overs to himself again. He cannot get the last ball away, though, and so Humphries is exposed to Williams. He plays two deliveries back to the bowler and each time blows out his cheeks in relief. Each time the fielders rise from the crouch, silently and taut. There is no joking now; the first specks of rain are in the air and Northamptonshire can feel the weather, as well as precious time, breathing down their necks. Williams bowls again, the fielders settle with their talons greedy for a catch. Humphries goes forward again nervously, the ball flies off the edge and Larkins, rising as on springs, has it in his hand. It is five o'clock, one hour left for play, and Worcester are 72 for 6. The momentum of the attack has been established again. It can be done, it can be done, even with D'Oliveira there, even now that he is joined by Norman Gifford, OBE, who never gave any game away and won that medal for playing hard. Gifford sees the over out, all bat and pads and trusting to luck. D'Oliveira takes over and patiently negotiates the time it takes for the biggest and blackest cloud in sight to drift cumbersomely from the east. At ten past five, Cook looks over his shoulder and suspects the worst from that cloud. In another five minutes it is overhead and casts such darkness over the County Ground that the umpires have no option but to call the players off. Before they have reached the pavilion a heavy drizzle starts, which goes on until long after the match might have been won and lost.

Thus Northants are confounded by weather when victory was almost within their grasp. A famous victory it would have been, too, taken so unexpectedly after lunch on the last of three days. A match so evenly contested, however, could have had no better ending than this, with the honours shared and the prize withheld from either side. It has been absorbing from the start, even when the play has been soft and slow. No wonder Neville Cardus saw cricket and music hand in hand, with crescendo and diminuendo patterning both and with, this past three days, vivid and moody solo passages on the bat. I can see how a Northamptonshire partisan might be left querulous in the end. But don't let anyone ever tell me that a drawn game must be a pointless and a boring thing.

## NORTHAMPTONSHIRE—*First Innings*

| | |
|---|---|
| W. LARKINS not out | 170 |
| G. COOK c Humphries b Pridgeon | 25 |
| D. S. STEELE c Hemsley b Cumbes | 6 |
| R. G. WILLIAMS lbw Gifford | 17 |
| P. WILLEY c Humphries b Holder | 24 |
| T. J. YARDLEY not out | 45 |
| Extras (b 4, lb 13, nb 8) | 25 |
| | |
| Total (for 4, 100 overs) | 312 |

Fall of wickets: 79, 97, 150, 185.

Bowling: HOLDER 23–1–59–1; PRIDGEON 23–4–64–1; CUMBES 16–1–70–1; GIFFORD 21–7–47–1; D'OLIVEIRA 1–0–3–0; PATEL 16–5–44–0.

## *Second Innings*

| | |
|---|---|
| W. LARKINS lbw Holder | 11 |
| G. COOK b Gifford | 21 |
| D. S. STEELE c Patel b Gifford | 117 |
| R. G. WILLIAMS st Humphries b Gifford | 46 |
| P. WILLEY c Neale b Patel | 10 |
| T. J. YARDLEY c Humphries b Cumbes | 3 |
| I. RICHARDS not out | 18 |
| G. SHARP c Humphries b Pridgeon | 13 |
| R. G. CARTER not out | 8 |
| Extras (b 3, lb 4, nb 11) | 18 |
| | |
| Total (for 7, declared) | 265 |

Fall of wickets: 18, 57, 179, 199, 212, 224, 251.

Did not bat: T. M. Lamb, B. J. Griffiths.

Bowling: HOLDER 24–6–54–1; PRIDGEON 12–1–42–1; CUMBES 14–5–33–1; GIFFORD 36–10–67–3; PATEL 18–5–42–1; D'OLIVEIRA 5–1–13–0.

## WORCESTERSHIRE—*First Innings*

| | |
|---|---:|
| G. M. TURNER c Cook b Willey | 127 |
| J. A. ORMROD c Sharp b Lamb | 65 |
| P. A. NEALE c Steele b Lamb | 74 |
| E. J. O. HEMSLEY not out | 31 |
| B. L. D'OLIVEIRA not out | 2 |
| Extras (b 1, lb 3, nb 5) | 9 |
| Total (for 3, 100 overs) | 308 |

Fall of wickets: 163, 233, 301.

Bowling: GRIFFITHS 25–2–85–0; LAMB 24–4–72–2; WILLEY 27–6–65–1; CARTER 7–1–17–0; STEELE 11–0–31–0; WILLIAMS 6–0–31–0.

## *Second Innings*

| | |
|---|---:|
| G. M. TURNER c Sharp b Griffiths | 2 |
| J. A. ORMROD lbw Griffiths | 16 |
| P. A. NEALE c Cook b Willey | 19 |
| E. J. O. HEMSLEY lbw Griffiths | 8 |
| B. L. D'OLIVEIRA not out | 30 |
| D. N. PATEL c Cook b Willey | 1 |
| D. J. HUMPHRIES c Larkins b Williams | 0 |
| N. GIFFORD not out | 0 |
| Extras (nb 1) | 1 |
| Total (for 6) | 77 |

Fall of wickets: 2, 38, 42, 50, 57, 72
Did not bat: V. A. Holder, A. P. Pridgeon, J. Cumbes.
Bowling: GRIFFITHS 11–2–33–3; LAMB 5–1–13–0; WILLEY 17–8–26–2; WILLIAMS 11.1–7–7–1.
Umpires: C. Cook and J. Van Geloven.
Match drawn: Northamptonshire 5 points, Worcestershire 5 points.

# Second Test Match

*June 16, 17 and 19*                    *Lord's*
### ENGLAND v PAKISTAN

PAKISTAN HAVE COME TO LORD'S WITH A DEPRESSING record, and this is partly due to exceedingly bad luck. Since arriving in April they have not won a game, and no team in England has suffered more from the awful weather of this year. Out of the first hundred hours of potential play on their tour, they lost something like seventy hours because of rain. They were therefore very short of match practice when they went into the First Test at Edgbaston a fortnight ago, but that does not wholly explain England's victory by an innings and 57 runs. It happens to be a sad fact of Pakistan's cricketing life that, since Mr Packer skimmed off their cream in the persons of Asif, Imran, Majid, Mushtaq and Zaheer, they are not half the side that contested a rubber here so stirringly four years ago. England have been marvellously fortunate in finding replacements for their own lost Packer players, and Pakistan have not been able to match them in this. True, they drew the winter series with the Englishmen in Pakistan, but the inexperience of the newcomers has been exposed away from the hot sun and baked pitches of their own land, and our weather this season has prevented them from learning how to adapt. It is quite consistent with the way things have gone for Pakistan this past few weeks that they have had to pick a team for Lord's without their most effective pace bowler, Sarfraz, who is absent hurt; and they will not have been astonished when the first day's play here is washed out without a ball being bowled.

The deluge begins just before the umpires are due to walk out, and spectators whose seats have been booked in the open air retreat to the covered portions of the stands and wait patiently for nothing to happen. Resigned figures in plastic macs read *Off-Licence News* more thoroughly than usual to pass the time. There is much speculation about who is explaining the hiatus to the television audience from the commentary box, where an arc light glares out of the gloom that otherwise suffuses the ground. A dozen chaps who have lugged a prodigious amount of wine and pâté, beer and salad and french bread up to the back rows of the Mound Stand, get on with their office party and become quite jolly by mid-afternoon. Someone keeps telling us by loudspeaker that "both teams and umpires are anxious that play shall *commence* as quickly as possible" and that the umpires will inspect the wicket "as soon as the rain *ceases*", making me wish I had a megaphone so that I might ask him whether he has never heard of "start" and "stop". The weather, however, doesn't let up for a minute. Even the geraniums near the Grace Gates, which have supplanted the tulips of spring, are wilting a little under all this wet. The cricket museum does a roaring trade and begins to smell like a laundry as its customers peer and steam. Lord's, on Test Match Thursday, hisses with rain and clinks with the sound of water trickling down drains.

Friday comes fine and warm, but the playing area is so sodden that cricket does not start until 12.15. While Jim Fairbrother and his mates struggle to get the boggier patches dry, crowds clog the paths around the practice ground and watch the cricketers make their own preparations for the fray. The Pakistanis are simply having a knock-up in twos and threes, some of them not even bothering to use the nets, but the Englishmen are involved in sterner stuff. The team's physiotherapist appears to be bent on pulling Willis limb from limb, hauling an arm from its socket one minute, forcing one of the bowler's feet high above his head the next, but if Willis survives this treatment it will doubtless produce the loosest bowling action we have ever seen. Gooch and Brearley, Radley, Botham and Roope are taking it in turns to give three at a time some slip practice with sharp balls off the edge and it is clear that, whichever man is using the bat, he is uncomfortable in this role, so completely is instinct against making such a stroke in real play. The rest of the squad are touching toes and going through other gymnastic routines before Bob Taylor has them catching high balls from a distance. Never before have I seen a bunch of cricketers so thoroughly organised in purely athletic drills before a match; and I don't think I've ever seen another distinction between two sides. As the Englishmen break up and cross the path, to head for the pavilion across the great green plateau of Lord's, each of them ignores the small boys thrusting out autograph books and pens. Most of the Pakistanis sign, and some of them look pleased to have been asked.

The ground is by no means full, but it is crowded enough to transmit excitement as we await the start. People find their seats with a sense of urgency, as they rarely do outside a Test. They deploy their victuals carefully so that, when these are needed, they can reach out a hand without taking their eyes from the game. They scan pavilion balconies with glasses, as soon as they have settled down, eager to see who's who and doing what. "'E's putting a lot of weight on these days," a West Country voice informs its neighbour, after spotting John Arlott in the press box. "Can't miss 'im." A cheer salutes the announcement that England have won the toss. Another signals the emergence of the umpires through the Long Room door. As the Pakistanis flow down the pavilion steps, clapping surges like a wave round the circle of the ground. A loud cheer follows, when the England openers come out, but it quickly subsides into a choral murmur of surprise, for this is the strangest-looking Brearley any of us have seen. We have become accustomed to him in that unique protective cricket cap with flaps. Today it has been abandoned in favour of a white appliance with a grille, and this is nothing less than the crash helmet American footballers wear. Well, we shall see; though I wonder whether the batsman himself will be able to see the ball as clearly as he should, with one of those bars crossing the end of his nose, which seems likely to distract as much as someone moving behind the bowler's arm.

For a team so soundly beaten in Birmingham, Pakistan begin the Second Test much better than they could have expected. They set a tight field and it is impetuous; when Gooch puts Sikander to deep square leg, two fieldsmen race for the ball so heedless of each other that, as they converge, Javed is felled by a perfect sliding tackle from Talat Ali. In the next over Brearley is blatantly lbw making no stroke, a man sadly out of form with the bat, who knows that fine captaincy alone cannot indefinitely keep him in this England team. Perhaps he didn't see that ball properly, because he removes the awful helmet before he is halfway to the pavilion, something he never did when he wore his other protective gear. For a few minutes Radley swings at the medium pace as though he is going to do it some harm; but then he mistimes Liaqat and puts a prentice catch into the covers, and England are 19 for 2. The anticipation that clenches the ground so quickly in the game is partly born of our surprise that Pakistan's limited resources should have so effectively broken through; but it is equally the prospect of Gower batting with his back to the wall that has us alert for what comes next. He has come to Lord's as our new golden boy, with a handsome 58 in the First Test after a spectacular century in the one-day Prudential match with Pakistan at the Oval. As long as I can remember, England have been looking for a left-handed batsman of the highest class, an enduring linchpin of the national side, as Barber, Pullar and Richardson never quite were. This season, at last, noses have begun to twitch at the scent of Leicestershire's young cub, and already there have been ecstatic headlines proclaiming Gower Power and the like.

The classical beauty of his stroke-making has stamped itself on all our minds before this game, but we have not yet seen whether it is equalled by his nerve: only once, in three international innings, has he come in with fewer than 100 runs on the board, with 60 for 2 at the Oval when he made his 114 not out. He walks out today gently, with great delicacy of step, shoulders leaning slightly forward as though his hands were clasped behind his back. He is slim, he has a froth of curly blond hair that his mother must still adore, and I have a sneaking suspicion that he calls everyone else on the England side "sir". He looks as if he was taught very early in life never to draw attention to himself and he surveys the field around him very briefly, as though he doesn't want to keep us waiting any longer. Then he swats the first ball over the slips to the boundary as easily as Clive Lloyd might, pulls the third past mid-wicket for another 4 and, by the end of that first over, has caught up with Gooch's score of 9. Evidently, David Gower has nerve.

And this morning he shows us all his class again. He employs almost all the strokes, from drive to glance, from hook to cut, but when he is not playing them he has a rare quality of stillness while he waits for the bowler's next turn. The distinctive things about his batting are its neatness, its air of total calm, its economy of effort and its fluent movement from quick back-lift to untrammelled follow-through. He does not appear to hit any ball with great power, even when it flies to the boundary as though from a catapult. He has applied the surface of the bat with such perfect timing to the ball that it is the bowler's energy, and not his own, which is consumed in Gower's appetite for runs. The science of ballistics is thus harnessed to the study of geometry, and natural grace exalts the result into the batsman's finest art.

The reassuring figure of Gooch works stolidly at the other end. He is built like a guardsman, and that expressionless face with its black moustache surely saw service in England's old imperial wars, defending Rorke's Drift and marching up the Khyber Pass. He has been readmitted to England's ranks, after that short and stumbled trot three years ago, because the imponderable Boycott is still in pain and because Wood did not do well enough in three innings against Pakistan for a man of his age with not a lot of future left. He is a hitter of the ball who puts all his beef behind both cut and drive. When Sikander lets him have a bouncer, Gooch shifts his head a fraction but otherwise does not budge, and I don't suppose he'd do more than grunt if the ball hit him square between the eyes. In these two batsmen, in Leicester and his worthy cousin Essex, England are served by rapier and broadsword out there, and from that parlous beginning safer ground is swiftly reached. Runs come at one a minute and, before 50 is posted, Wasim Bari decides it is time for a change. He swaps Sikander for Mudassar and, at last, sends more than one man to the boundary. It takes the Pakistan captain several minutes to discharge this responsibility before he resumes duty as wicketkeeper; instructing his bowlers will become a regular feature of this day, accompanied by sweeping gestures to all parts of the field which come straight from the repertoire of a policeman trying to sort out a traffic jam. The West Country man in N block, interested in all that goes on at Lord's, enlightens his neighbour on the form of colloquy between Wasim and his men. "They can talk English, you know." In this way, Pakistan is etched more clearly on the map of Wessex.

The adjustment, though, does not staunch the flow of runs and every time the ball goes over the ropes, the crowd bellows its pleasure. This is *England* forging ahead in an international match and no one, for the moment, is giving a thought to the quality of the attack which is not, alas, above the second-rate. Nor is much of the fielding worthy of a Test. Gooch hits one just wide of Mohsin at midwicket and the fieldsman turns, chases the ball and stops it some yards from the edge of the field. Twice he stoops to pick it up and fails both times. When, at last, he has it in his hand, he throws it straight at Wasim's feet; then collapses in giggles at the mess, which has cost Pakistan a couple of runs. If either Randall or Barlow (both unable to get into this England side) had been fielding there, two runs would have been impossible and probably a single wouldn't have been on.

And yet the perfection of cricket asserts itself a little after lunch when fortunes are suddenly, against all likelihood, reversed. Wasim Bari has resorted to spin and musters close fielders in front of the bat. Javed takes stance at silly mid-off in a sunhat, but Sadiq calls for armour before facing any peril that may issue from the other side of the batting strip. He himself sees something ridiculous in the helmet brought out to him by Pakistan's twelfth man: putting it on he swivels, bares his teeth behind its bars, and pretends to tommy gun the Tavern crowd. He gets his laugh but, for once in my life, I wish the response were less friendly than that. The use of helmets by batsmen against dangerous pace may be debatable, but I don't think there's any excuse for close fieldsmen wearing them at all. Fielding in the so-called "silly" positions, after all, is not merely an act of courage which deserves applause when it is truly that and not a half-hearted pretence. It is also an intimidation of the batsman, an emotional pressure which can only be justified if the fieldsmen are prepared to yield their own security in return, and as much of a distraction as the presence of a spectator alongside a grandmaster's chessboard. The use of an artificial aid to increase the already heavy odds in favour of the bowling side and against the solitary bat is to tip the fine balance between what is fair play and what is not. I don't suppose for a minute that, today, Sadiq has contemplated his helmet in such terms. It may or may not be that his pantomime has disturbed the concentration of Gower and Gooch. The fact is that a flaw now appears in the batting of both (and it is this which makes each innings beautiful, where it might have been merely faultless). First Gooch goes back to Wasim Raja's top spinner and gets his leg before. Without another run added, Gower plays across the line of a ball from Iqbal Qasim and is bowled: and England are 120 for 4.

The Pakistanis hunch fiercely around the incoming batsmen, anxious to press the quick advantage home. Time after time they appeal for catches off bump-balls, but Roope has the nerve a batsman needs to fight his way out of the encircling movements of the foe. He drives and sweeps as though close fieldsmen were not there to profit from his slightest miscalculation in putting bat to ball. He will test their own nerves to stay where they are and, from half the balls he receives, Javed and Sadiq are forced to duck and jump one-legged to reduce the chances of being struck. They do hold fast, though, because at the other end Miller is struggling to hold his own, the perfect quarry for such an ambush as theirs. With glasses you can see the grim set of Miller's face as he strives to smother each ball before it can play him tricks, and the naked eye can sense the agonised uncertainty in his reaching out while, almost within touch on either side of his bat, those two pairs of hands are flexed like talons ready to clutch. For a few endless deliveries poor Miller gropes for salvation, his predicament made more obvious by the way Roope turns the tables on the ambush when the bowling comes to him. There can be only one outcome unless a batsman so confined suddenly discovers a missing element in his play and joins in the assault upon the bowler and his field; and Miller can make no such discovery today. By no more than a whisker, perhaps, he fails to do what he must do if he is to survive Iqbal Qasim's wavering spin. The ball flicks from bat to pad and up into the air, Javed uncoils from his crouch, quarry becomes victim, and England are 134 for 5.

Pakistan can forget the humiliations of Edgbaston now. Let Javed and Sadiq and the spinners keep their pressures up to take another wicket soon, and England's first innings total may be well within their own batsmen's reach. Botham's frame of mind, however, is evident the moment he steps clear of the pavilion gate. He flails the air with his bat, on mighty rotations of his arm, and he is halfway to the wicket before he desists. This is more than a matter of thoroughly loosening up: it is a message to Pakistan that another Miller is not on the way, that pure aggression is now heading for the crease. Roope, with 14 runs already notched, is in no need of Botham's cue but he takes it all the same and greets his new partner by hitting Wasim Raja into the Grandstand for 6. Sadiq only just moves in time to escape a blow that might have taken his head off, helmet and all. In Qasim's next over, Botham himself strikes an identical blow, and from that moment the ambush prudently begins to retreat. For a little while longer, English hearts will still be in suspense, as the occasional ball tests the batsmen's mettle to the full; and, mindful of the score, neither of them at the start of their partnership is ready to take the calculated risk. But every loose ball is punished hard, and gradually Pakistan's expectations fall.

Roope steadily carves a substantial score and he is still in full pelt when tea comes at 187 for 5. But, more and more, it is Botham who gladdens Lord's in the heat of late afternoon. Here is England's greatest gain since Kerry Packer's blandishments enticed that quartet of regulars from the national team. His rise to international rank has been pure *Boy's Own Paper* ever since that day in 1974 when he had his teeth smashed by Andy Roberts, refused to leave the field, and went on to win the match for Somerset with two 6s into the bargain – and him only eighteen years old. He bats the way small boys dream of batting, with his shoulders opened wide whenever he decides to hit, with great swings and sweeps of his blade that send the ball bounding past fieldsmen who can only stand and gape. Where David Gower touches and strokes and elegantly clips the ball, Ian Botham bangs it about with muscularity and lust. The one excites the mind and shyly discloses grace; the other makes the heart leap and truculently has his way. When Botham is in the mood of this innings, when he is faced by bowlers who are unable to turn him off, he takes almost all attention from whoever is batting at the other end. We are tempted to watch Botham merely backing up so that we, too, can savour the pause before his assault goes on. When Roope drives once more to extra cover and is caught, his downfall is but an incident in Botham's progress to more runs. This is unfair, but there it is.

When the last hour of play comes, Botham has long since dispersed the field and Wasim Bari's point duty seems to be taking place at a particularly busy junction. He marshals his men this way and that at every over's end in his attempts to put them somewhere near the path of Botham's next few strokes. Some of the traffic answers back, the captain gesticulates even more, and David Constant accepts the opportunity to sprawl on the grass until the wheels begin to move again. But whatever field is set, it cannot contain Botham today. Still the ball reaches the boundary, so swiftly that no man more than ten yards from where it crosses the ropes has a hope of cutting it off. Botham's exertions are so great that the right leg of his flannels splits under the strain. Gower runs out with Sellotape to preserve modesty but Botham takes one look at the stuff and grandly waves it back; and continues to weigh into the ball with such gusto that it becomes possible that its seam, too, will give way. He loses Bob Taylor, faithful liegeman propping up the other end, and Sikander is on a hat-trick when he takes Old with the next ball. But, again, these are only sub-plots while that central figure is still on stage. When the last over begins, Botham has reached 95; when play ends, he is 102 not out. He has scored those last runs with seven men standing on the boundaries of Lord's, and that is the best measurement of what he has done today. He has reduced the first innings of a Test Match, which is supposed to be such a majestic thing, to the level of a climax in the hectic Sunday League.

The Saturday crowd gathers in the hope of seeing him bat on in the same way when England continue at 309 for 8. He gets a couple off Sikander's first over, to the seven scored by Edmonds. Liaqat's first delivery is hit straight to the boundary with the arrogance of the night before. As the second ball comes down, Botham moves on to the back foot to give himself a mite more room for another savage blow but this time (thank God for mortal men) he drags the ball back into his stumps. His head goes back in disgust but the pavilion is already rising, tier by tier, to salve bruised pride with the acclaim that MCC men reserve for their most favoured sons. It is Edmonds and Willis who flog the Pakistan bowling for the rest of England's time – and the 40 runs they quickly add puts both bowlers and wicket in their proper light. There is no reason at all why batsmen with the proven abilities of Sadiq, Javed and Haroon should not get a bagful of runs today, even though there is muggy warmth to help the pacemen's swing when the Pakistan innings starts. And yet, long before lunch, it is clear that England's score of 364 is going to be well beyond the tourists' reach.

Their bogey (if we are to dismiss everything from English weather to Pakistan politics from the count) is Bob Willis, who opens from the Nursery end. To any batsmen in the world, the Warwickshire bowler has become a disturbing sight as he races in from his distant mark. He runs all the way like a track athlete heading for the tape, upright and with both chin and breast determined to get there first; only the ticking of his hand behind the right hip distinguishes his sport from the other until the moment when he flings himself into the bowling of the ball. To genuinely fast bowling he has lately added a nasty habit of indiscriminate bouncers, one of which struck Iqbal Qasim in the face during the Birmingham Test, and it was this which produced an agreement between the two captains as to which men on either side at Lord's should not be subjected to such balls – Iqbal, Sikander and Liaqat for Pakistan, Hendrick (eventually made twelfth man) and Willis himself for England. Inevitably, perhaps, Sadiq begins the innings with crash helmet on his head while, behind his bat, no fewer than seven men crouch with cupped hands like a ring of beady seagulls hungrily picketing the beach.

They do not have to wait long to snatch the first bite. It takes Willis one over to loosen properly those extravagant limbs. Old serves up his own opener, drawing himself back like a bow just before crashing headlong into his last stride. From those twelve balls the Pakistan batsmen manage to cudgel 11 runs. Then Willis comes in again, pitches the ball short, Mudassar misjudges everything in trying to hook and Edmonds rises from the ring to gobble a gentle catch. This almost petrifies Sadiq and the next handful of runs come from Mohsin's bat. In his third over, Willis makes another ball lift. Sadiq's parrying defence sends the ball straight to Gooch, who is fifth in line of that baleful close field, but Gooch puts it down. Not a flicker of disturbance from Willis's face or his back as he lopes away to try again. He returns from the Nursery end with the very same delivery, which Sadiq plays with much the same shot. This time it is Botham, two along from Gooch, who goes for the ball; and makes no mistake.

Haroon comes to the crease with a reputation to repair. He pitched into the Englishmen so forcibly during their winter tour that he made Mr Packer's mouth water and is said to be bespoke for the gaudier life the moment this series is done. But the poor chap made only 3 and 4 in the shambles of Edgbaston, and he can probably imagine the carrot being suddenly whipped from under his nose unless he does better now, for he must know that World Series Cricket is not a charity for players, whatever Mr Packer and his underlings imply. Haroon therefore tries to attack the bowling as soon as he arrives. He even clouts Willis splendidly into the top row of the Grandstand for 6, and it says much about the temper of this crowd, who can identify a proper underdog when they see one, that this blow gets the biggest cheer of the match so far. A slashing 4 in the same over creates the same amount of noise; but that, for Haroon, is just about that. Moments before lunch he drives at Old, misses the ball, and hears the click of leather on stump.

We are scarcely settled back into our seats before Pakistan's innings lurches yet again. Javed, another man who may be playing for his Packer place, who only two years ago was a blazing new prodigy on the international scene, nervously pokes at Willis and is caught behind for a duck. The tourists are 41 for 4 and, with their established batsmen all but gone, on the edge of disaster. For the best part of an hour they manage to pull themselves up at the brink. Wasim Raja appears as swashbuckler in a beard, and Mohsin tensely cultivates a decent crop. In doubling the Pakistan score, they induce Brearley to make a bowling change, and it is the advent of Edmonds which finishes both of them off. First Raja goes, trying to sweep once too often. Then it is Mohsin's turn, tantalised too long, patience snapped, lashing out violently in the direction of mid-off, where Willis jerks and tumbles but still holds ball fiercely to his belt. From 96 for 6, Pakistan plummet horribly to their end, so demoralised by the time the eighth wicket falls that Sikander, on getting his first ball from Edmonds on the pad, automatically turns and begins to walk, though the appeal has been half-hearted and the umpire has nothing to say. Edmonds, mind, is bowling his off-spin with control and fine deceit, as well as with the loveliest action of its kind since Richie Benaud had us under his spell. That high-elbowed clasp of the hands, that swirling arm and swerving hip; those mannerisms, too – the quick rub of the right fingers in the dirt as he walks back past the stumps, and the lick at the left fingertips before he gets to the turn. I could watch Phil Edmonds bowl at nothing more responsive than a brick wall and still be glad to have seen. As a player, though, he deserves worthier opponents than have faced him today. A side out for 105 on a batting strip like this is lacking character as much as skill.

The second innings starts even more wretchedly than the first, when Sadiq is caught behind with only an extra on the board – no start at all for a team following-on 259 runs behind. At that moment it is conceivable that the Second Test Match will be over by Saturday night, for tea is yet to come and it will take more than the catering of Lord's to fortify this side till close of play. From somewhere, however, Pakistan find enough resolution to see them through the day. They are doubtless helped by the weather at last, no more than their due, for the sun is booming hotly again and the mugginess is gone and Chris Old is no longer able to produce balls that curve through the air like bananas. More gratefully, perhaps, Pakistan see little of Willis this time round, for he keeps leaving the field with cramp and lets them have only four overs of you-know-what. Mudassar plays very quietly, Mohsin solves problems at the other end, the score creeps gently up the board. Some spectators begin to doze, others ferry quantities of beer from the Tavern to the stands, and a man with binoculars thinks he identifies Jim Laker behind plate glass, carefully droppin' his word endin's for the benefit of watchers on TV. Then Botham comes on and manages to lift one out of the sleepy pitch, and Mudassar is not quick enough to get his bat out of the ball's flight to Bob Taylor's gloves. Perhaps Haroon declines to face a second death in the afternoon; at any rate, it is Talat Ali who vaults three places in the batting order to come in next. If this is a strategy, it serves Pakistan better than anything in this match before. Spectacles glinting with new light, Talat plays cricket worthy of the name, hitting any ball offering scope, studiously blocking everything that bears a threat. Mohsin gradually emerges from his contemplative's hood, begins to play shots, too, once jumps out to Edmonds and cracks him for 6 over the long-on ropes. They do not take command, these two, but with an unbroken partnership of 51 in eighty minutes, tonight they restore an amount of dignity that had been lost somewhere along the way this afternoon. Brearley revolves his bowlers once or twice and Miller's flat trajectories come skimming down. They are inexpensive and they turn a bit, but they do not take their men, in spite of encouragement from the Tavern crowd. When Talat and Mohsin came together, the beer started singing "When The Saints Go Marching In", but by close of play the chorus has degenerated into a straggle of shouts and burps. Pakistan have reached 96 for two and it is the sound of a bagpiper's "Amazing Grace" that cuts above the tramp of homebound feet behind the stands.

Monday comes gloriously; but miserably, too. Not a cloud to be seen, a perfect day for a game, and crocodiles of schoolboys being chivvied into place all over the ground for six hours of cricket-watching in the middle of term. Without them, though, it would be a pretty thin crowd, not much more than you would expect to see at a mid-week county game. Sadly for the schoolboys, the cricket lasts less than two hours and Pakistan's batsmen are by and large only a lesson in how not to bat. But at least those who have turned up at Lord's see history made by Ian Botham, though this happens almost accidentally. After Willis and Old have opened with an over apiece they decide to change ends, and Botham comes on to bowl half a dozen balls from the Nursery end so that they can make their swap. He has Talat Ali in so much trouble from the start that Brearley shrewdly decides to let him be; and there he stays for the rest of the match. Willis gets

Mohsin to put a catch into the slips as soon as he takes up Old's position at the pavilion end; but every wicket falls to the Somerset all-rounder after that. Talat edges one into the slips, Haroon loses two stumps, Wasim Raja miscues and simply pats the ball back whence it came, while Pakistan's captain almost ruptures himself trying to reach a wide half volley and deserves to be caught.

So it goes on, while Botham simply bowls flat out, accurately most of the time, and gets his outswingers to bend so much (surprisingly on such a brazen day) that Taylor twice throws himself full length and still doesn't stop the ball going past. There is a great cheer from the schoolboys when Mohsin's wicket falls, but the procession of batsmen becomes so regular and frequent that the cheers turn to groans, as the Third Form sees its day's outing severely curtailed. By the time Botham has worked his way down to Sikander, there never was such a silent gang of partisans at Lord's with England so powerfully on top. At this point a loud and dramatic hiss explodes from the second balcony of the pavilion, which is as good a comment as any on the one-sided proceedings below, but which turns out to be television equipment giving way under the strain. Only Javed is putting up any sort of show and, when the ninth wicket falls, he abandons defiance, swipes out at a few and finally is caught. Pakistan have lost eight wickets before lunch for 43 runs and Botham's feat this morning has been to take seven of them for only 14. His analysis for the innings, 8 for 34, represents the most successful piece of bowling by an Englishman in Tests since Laker's destruction of Australia at Old Trafford in 1956. In the entire history of Test cricket, no man until today had taken eight wickets in an innings and scored a century in the match as well.

And yet there is no sense of attending an historic event. England v Pakistan has been a mismatch again, what should have been a five-day Test has lasted less than half that long, and Botham's triumph is one that only the record books will tell; we shall not bore our children with all its details and distant light in our eyes. It is clear that England need no longer lament the loss of Tony Greig, who wouldn't now be able to get into the side even if he were in a position to try. Add the discovery of Gower and the potential renaissance of Gooch, and it is possible to argue that Mr Packer's intrusion has done rather more good than harm to our national side. But our new young men have scarcely been tried by what they have so far faced; only if they do as well as this against Bobby Simpson's young Australians in the winter shall we know their sterling worth. This has been little more than the sideshow before the real contest starts. And lunch was taken early on the third day, watching the ducks in Regent's Park.

## ENGLAND—*First Innings*

| | |
|---|---|
| J. M. BREARLEY lbw Liaqat | 2 |
| G. A. GOOCH lbw Raja | 54 |
| C. T. RADLEY c Mohsin b Liaqat | 8 |
| D. I. GOWER b Qasim | 56 |
| G. R. J. ROOPE c Mohsin b Qasim | 69 |
| G. MILLER c Javed b Qasim | 0 |
| I. T. BOTHAM b Liaqat | 108 |
| R. W. TAYLOR c Mudassar b Sikander | 10 |
| C. M. OLD c Mohsin b Sikander | 0 |
| P. H. EDMONDS not out | 36 |
| R. G. D. WILLIS b Mudassar | 18 |
| Extras (lb, 2, nb 1) | 3 |
| Total | 364 |

Fall of Wickets: 5, 19, 120, 120, 134, 252, 290, 190, 324.
Bowling: SIKANDER 27–3–115–2; LIAQAT 18–1–18–3; MUDASSAR 4.2–0–16–1; QASIM 30–5–101–3; RAJA 12–3–49–1.

## PAKISTAN—*First Innings*

| | |
|---|---|
| SADIQ MOHAMMAD c Botham b Willis | 11 |
| MUDASSAR NAZAR c Edmonds b Willis | 1 |
| MOHSIN KHAN c Willis b Edmonds | 31 |

| | |
|---|---:|
| HAROON RASHID b Old | 15 |
| JAVED MIANDAD c Taylor b Willis | 0 |
| WASIM RAJA b Edmonds | 28 |
| TALAT ALI c Radley b Edmonds | 2 |
| WASIM BARI c Brearley b Willis | 0 |
| IQBAL QASIM b Willis | 0 |
| SIKANDER BAKHT c Brearley b Edmonds | 4 |
| LIAQAT ALI not out | 4 |
| Extras (nb 9) | 9 |
| Total | 105 |

Fall of wickets: 11, 22, 40, 41, 84, 96, 97, 97, 105.
Bowling: WILLIS 13–1–47–5; OLD 10–3–26–1; BOTHAM 5–2–17–0; EDMONDS 8–6–6–4.

## Second Innings

| | |
|---|---:|
| SADIQ MOHAMMAD c Taylor b Willis | 0 |
| MUDASSAR NAZAR c Taylor b Botham | 10 |
| MOHSIN KHAN c Roope b Willis | 46 |
| TALAT ALI c Roope b Botham | 40 |
| HAROON RASHID b Botham | 4 |
| JAVED MIANDAD c Gooch b Botham | 22 |
| WASIM RAJA c and b Botham | 1 |
| WASIM BARI c Taylor b Botham | 2 |
| SIKANDER BAKHT c Roope b Botham | 1 |
| IQBAL QASIM b Botham | 0 |
| LIAQAT ALI not out | 0 |
| Extras (b 1, lb 3, nb 4, w 5) | 13 |
| Total | 139 |

Fall of wickets: 1, 45, 100, 108, 114, 119, 121, 130, 130.
Bowling: WILLIS 10–2–26–2; OLD 15–4–36–0; BOTHAM 20.5–6–34–8; EDMONDS 12–4–21–0; MILLER 9–3–9–0.
Umpires: W. L. Budd and D. J. Constant.
England won by an innings and 120 runs.

# Village Championship

FEW THINGS ARE MORE DEEPLY ROOTED IN THE COLLECTIVE imagination of the English than the village cricket match. It stirs a romantic illusion about the rustic way of life, it suggests a tranquil and unchanging order in an age of bewildering flux, and it persuades a lot of townsfolk that this is where they would rather be. People who reckon to be bored stiff by any form of the game will pause, at the first glimpse of white flannels on the other side of a hedge, and give those absorbed figures the same dreamy attention they otherwise spend only on scrapbooks of the past. They are minded of a folklore with Squire and Parson and Blacksmith meeting as almost equals in a green and pleasant land, and this has a more powerful grip on the English soul than any conventional haughtiness towards flannelled fools. Village cricket occupies a comforting place in the nostalgic tapestry of the island race – but its closest neighbour is perhaps the spectre of young subalterns leading their men across Flanders mud, swinging a cane (or even a cricket bat) blithely as they make their way towards the enemy guns. The writers, of course, have done as much as anyone to perpetuate the myth, especially when they have been trying to tickle their readers by poking fun at the game. The cliché observation is perfectly true: it is indeed remarkable that cricket has inspired a greater wealth and quality of literature than any other sport in the world, a large proportion of it composed around the English village match. Few authors will have written fiction about our rural life without admitting cricket to at least the margins of their books.

The fact that part of the image does not always, or even

very often nowadays, coincide with reality is almost beside the point. Squires and blacksmiths are in pretty short supply, but the village game's vitality has been obvious ever since 1972, when the first national knockout competition was organised for teams from rural communities with a population of 2,500 or less (and no one with first-class cricket experience allowed to play, please note, unless he is over sixty years old). When last year's championship final took place, more than 5,000 spectators turned up to watch it on a Monday at Lord's, and when this year's long journey to Mecca began, 836 village teams had enlisted to play each other throughout England, Scotland and Wales. By the middle of this month, Aston Rowant (population 700) had beaten Ardington by 61 runs and Tiddington (population 800) had disposed of Shrivenham by 3 wickets, thus earning today's contest for the Group Final, to decide which of them shall carry Oxfordshire's hopes into the regional sixth round. Scarcely a man on either side conforms to the mythical composition of the village team. Tiddington have a farm labourer batting at Number Ten, but are otherwise served by a couple of schoolboys, a brace of estate surveyors, an accountant, a bank clerk, a draughtsman, a laboratory technician, a man who works on the shop floor at British Leyland, and a chap who describes himself as a building trainee. Aston Rowant's fortunes are in the hands of five engineers (civil and otherwise), two employees of a gramophone recording company, an estimator, a railway clerk, a long-distance lorry driver and a teacher. The home team does, however, have the backing of Squire, president of the club and owner of the ground, an ex-colonel with a hyphenated name. You can see the roofline of his manor, standing among trees half a mile away on the other side of the road.

There are two Oxfordshires and this is not the Cotswold part, all thatched and limestoned and hollyhocks by the door. The parish of Aston Rowant lies under a wooded ridge of the Chilterns, and it is mostly brick and pantiles and slate round here, pretty enough but not in the chocolate-box way. There is a church with a Norman nave and some heavy restoration by various Victorian hands, though it was probably Cromwell's men who left that dunt in the floor by the chancel steps, where there was once a large brass commemorating Sir Hugh le Blount, who died in 1314. Both church and its sustaining wriggle of cottages are tucked into a byway, off a B-road, and the nearest signpost does you the kindness of pointing out that down there lies *Aston Rowant (only)*, with its staddle stones imported from the other Oxfordshire by the incumbent villagers of 1978, who are – as their cricket team suggests – mostly of the mobile middle class. The ground, in fact, is a mile or more away, on the edge of the next village, which is Kingston Blount. That is a Kingston farmer's barn rising beyond mid-wicket, its asbestos roof already sheltering much baled hay; and it is his tractor that starts to mow the next meadow as the players turn up at the cricket field, where a tree by the gate bears a hand-made notice announcing the match.

Many supporters arrive, too, with memories of Aston v Tiddington stretching back the best part of a hundred years, and a lot of folk have come the seven or eight miles from Tiddington way, wearing blue T-shirts with a fox stencilled across the chest. Some time before the match starts, fifty or sixty cars are parked under the hedges that border most of the ground, and alongside the wooden fence that separates a corner of the cricket from a paddock where horses (bred for hunting, not the farm) browse beneath chestnuts that give shade from the sun. Inside the breeze-block shed that acts as pavilion, Aston ladies are cutting sandwiches for tea, while the bar begins to slake the Sunday thirst from its range of optics and pumps, and its barrel of real ale with a proper bung and tap. Someone thoughtfully draws a pint for the Aston scorer, who is sharpening pencils and smoothing pages at his little table just outside. Squire drops by, military figure in tweed, and has a word with scorer before going in to encourage his lads, but if Parson has also turned up this afternoon he must have left his dog collar down at the Rectory after Matins were done. Players emerge for a knock-up, with "1st XI" branded in poker-work on the back of some bats. People sprawl on the grass within reach of the bar, begin to banter, give ear to a baggy little man in elderly grey flannels who is trying to remember something that happened round here on VE Day – "No, at Coronation it were." The captains toss and, winning it, Tiddington put the home side in. The umpires walk to the middle, self-consciousness covered by authority's flapping white coat, one of which has a red collar and may have seen other duty in the milkman's trade. Its owner gives Aston's opener leg and middle, calls "play" to the bowler at the Chiltern end, and the village match begins.

It starts as carefully as a professional contest, though Aston's batsmen must know that this wicket is as safe as they come, with none of the topographical features that are supposed to add interest and uncertainty to the rural bowler's game. The entire playing area, indeed, is beautifully cut and rolled, and I've seen county grounds where they'd be glad to call the plough in if they could then have turf like this. Nor is there anything casual in the way these cricketers have dressed, with everyone in whites (or at least in cream) and the only curiosity the farmer's boy, who is down in the gully with long tresses contained by a blue headband, which gives him a piratical or a Pueblo air. For an over or two the openers are content to nudge and push, but then Number Two tries to force the pace and gets caught behind with 16 runs on Aston's account. Number One's watchword has been patience so far, taking no risks, keen on staying put, very correct in everything he does, a regular Boycott of a man. But with his first partner gone he begins to play shots and soon Aston's score is fairly skimming along. The third man, Howells, makes a groggy start, nearly swinging himself over the Chilterns in an effort to connect with a wide long hop. Then he aims a blow at the covers, from which he gets a single astern between his legs. Test batsmen have been known to do the same thing, though, and presently Howells comes into the game. By the time raffle tickets are being sold to the crowd (three for 10p) for a bottle of Scotch and a chocolate gâteau, Aston Rowant have made 50 without further loss.

Boundaries begin to flow, mostly from McQueen, Aston's Number One. The ball comes crashing towards the pavilion, just as a toddler lurches on to the grass. "Keep him off that pitch, Ma," warns an Aston player, padded up, awaiting his turn. "Watch that ball. It'll knock his bloody head off." This is the only anxiety the locals have, now that McQueen is well into his stride. "That were a shaky old start for him," they all agree, settling more confidently into their ale. The Tiddington contingent are becoming thoughtful, but they are still in humour with the day. "Jammy old boy," says one, when a ball is chipped just over square leg's head and rolls away for 4. "Come on Rupert, you'll get there," as one of their own men goes galloping round the far boundary to cut off another hit. They can see this match tilting decisively Aston's way as the 100 goes up, and still no sign of another break. But then Howells is bowled, and his wicket is celebrated with another round of pints. This brings in the lorry driver, Aston's equivalent of the blacksmith in Macdonell's book, who came up to bowl "breasting the slope superbly like a mettlesome combination of Vulcan and Venus Anadyomene." He is a man of great stature who might do well in a wrestling bout, and the Tiddington crowd are much impressed with the swagger of his girth as he strides forth to bludgeon runs. "There must," says one T-shirt to another, "be an answer to that somewhere." It is odds on that if the batsman can only connect with the ball, he will put it out of sight. Opinion is that, when he is judged to have made 4 past the wicketkeeper to the hedge, this was caused not by a snick but by the powerful draught in an aerodynamic sweep of the bat.

A gust of laughter at the entrance to the bar, as the local policeman arrives. "I've heard reports," he says, "that they're selling duff beer in here, and I've just come to check up." Once he would have pedalled up that B-road on a Raleigh, with a helmet on his head, but he is car-borne these days, with a chequered cap and a walkie-talkie clipped to his lapel. He is still the village bobby, though, and spends the next half hour wandering round the ground, pausing with old ladies to ask them how do they do, chatting with the young chaps about the state of the game: affable constable carefully tending his patch. He watches the lorry driver clout another ball high into the air, hears Tiddington shout "Well done, Rupert, well done boy!" when it is caught, murmurs "Bad luck, Bill" with the other Aston folk when the batsman comes back. It is their captain's turn next. As he rises from his deck chair, he has a captain's word with the young fellow who will follow when another wicket goes. "If you're at the other end, keep your eye on me. Right?" Brian Close probably said something of the sort, the first season Ian Botham went to bat.

More wickets fall, as Aston Rowant's men try to cram as many runs as possible into the book before their 40 overs are done. Both lots of supporters cry encouragement to their men, dig each other in the ribs when something goes amiss for the other side. A bowler pulls up short, having swallowed a fly. "Should have had your dinner afore you came," bawls someone in the crowd, and a granny slaps her thighs, beside herself with glee. A Tiger Moth drones lazily above Oxfordshire's patchwork of fields, a blue kite wobbles into the sky over Kingston Blount, the tractor still cuts swathes in the next meadow, layering the ground with the new-mown smell. McQueen bats on, village hero by now, dazzling white figure dashing to and fro, creating an excitement of his own which is almost separate from that attending the course of the game. He reaches his century just before Aston's ration of overs is spent, with a walloping drive to the boundary that leaves bowler rueful, hands on hips. "Swing it!" shout Astonians at almost every ball bowled; and swing it their men do, until their time is done.

A big clap for McQueen as he comes in not out, glowing like an apple, his hair all sticky with sweat. "Well done, lads!" for the Tiddington men, who would have done very well if it hadn't been for him. They look ready for their tea, which is bubbling in the urn, but the bowlers pause first by the table outside, peer over the scorer's shoulder to see how their averages look. A small boy pulls tin plates off the scoreboard, puts them in order again for

Tiddington's knock. While the players munch sand-wiches, two men trundle the roller out to the middle. Like them, it is getting on a bit, squeaking and groaning as a wind pump will do when it hasn't seen the oilcan for rather too long. It is large and ponderous, with a hand-beam on either side, and the men lean into these or back against them like a pair of draught horses working on heavy clay. Everyone else lolls idly in the sun, except for a couple of youths by the meadow hedge, who are gunning up a motor-bike, cocky and proud, indifferent to the noise. A hundred yards away, a frown crosses the brow of a lady in brogues, who may already have seen more cricket than she really wishes to watch. Yesterday was spent observing her sons playing for their school. Today, for the benefit of two languid young things (house guests by the look), she is recalling all those years she spent in Tobago and advising them to go to Bermuda, not Barbados, if they must.

Benches are brought out, so that the teams may have their photographs taken after tea. The Tiddington side grin as the shutter clicks, though they cannot be all that sanguine when they must make 178 to win. Not many visitors have scored so many runs against Aston Rowant on this pitch, for this is a keen attack, with combative instincts sharpened since "friendly" cricket matches were abandoned in favour of competition in Oxfordshire's new Trinity League. No one is keener than the lorry driver, whose formidable figure is now arranged in pads and gloves behind the stumps where (wisely, perhaps) he disdains the ordinary wicketkeeper's crouch, adopting the more manoeuvrable stance of a right-angled bend. From this position he will rear up after every ball bowled, sometimes with a mighty roar, which probably under-mines the non-striker's nerve as effectively as a whale surfacing in the path of a dory on the Newfoundland Banks. It only requires steady bowling as counterpoint to this and Tiddington, it is clear, will have their work cut out.

They are struggling from the start, and this is not so much because they lose their openers quickly as because their batsmen find it hard to get the ball away for runs, even when they seem able to keep their wickets intact. By the time 15 overs have come down they have scored no more than 27 for 2, which means that they must knock 6 off each over for the rest of the game, and they never look like doing this. Long faces begin to set gloomily above Tiddington's share of the ale, and Number Three becomes the butt of all vexation issuing from the region of the bar. He is a man of deflections and tentative pushes, an accountant who believes in carefully totting up figures and keeping out of the red, when what Tiddington folk want is full-blooded swings. "He'll bat till Tuesday, will Rowland, for 20 runs," is the sort of comment they make with their side in this tardy state. But then they get a spot of action they could do without, when Number Three calls for a quick one and, though Tiddington's captain scuttles like a rabbit, he never nearly makes his ground before Aston's centurion at cover has thrown the wicket down. A chorus of groans below the Aston cheers, and "He wouldn't have made that with a skateboard on." The lorry driver punches the air with his fist, as footballers do when they have scored a goal, which is maybe why the lady in brogues changes from a Caribbean to a South American tack. Her cousin, it seems, is lately back from Argentina, with a report that they've had to put TV sets in all the factories so that the workers can see the World Cup. One of her house guests nods politely while he tries to take in cricket as well, but the other's eyes are fixed on a flock of birds, speckling the sky then curving into line, as they wheel and change plane over Kingston Blount.

Just after that run-out, Aston bring up a new bowler and the home supporters perk up even more, sure that this move means the end for Tiddington. "If 'e finds a length, 'e's 'appy," explains one, as the new man measures out his run with goosesteps. "Gauleiter's walk, isn't it?" says the scorer to no one in particular, a school-masterish man who is keeping a very neat book. The delivery is just as strange; half a dozen quick steps and a hop which takes this Goldie straight up into the air, the best part of a foot off the ground, while right arm comes down with a swish and the ball is bowled. It is effective enough, though, to take the next three wickets for only a scattering of runs and, at 42 for five, for a Tiddington fellow to sigh heavily and declare that it's all over now. The roars of laughter are all from the Aston supporters gathered round a man called Reg, whose blazer and Daks are faultlessly pressed, whose face beams perpetually with an obliging smile, and whose hair gleams as carefully as Denis Compton's used to in his Brylcreem days. Reg, one gathers, is a man who fancies a flutter now and then and, ever since he entered the cricket field when Aston were something like 75 for 1, people have been hailing him speculatively about the odds. Now, surrounded by cronies and admirers, he is the centre of much mirth, which he seems to provoke by not saying a word, merely by changing the angle or the direction of his grin. In its way this is as much a virtuoso performance as anything happening in the middle, where Number Three is still trying to balance Tiddington's books. He is involved in another run-out, to make the visitors 53 for 7; and then, in a decisive move, chops the next ball but four straight on to his own stumps. He does not look pleased as he comes striding back, and Tiddington supporters by the scoreboard try carefully not to catch his eye.

It is the farmer's boy who at last brings an heroic touch to the visitors' innings. He walks to the wicket with the tail of his headband streaming behind and with a wish-me-luck look on his amiable face. He swipes, with a kind of straight drive, at the first two balls he receives and gets a couple of runs off the second. Possibly deciding that a cross-batted clout might improve on this, he launches the whole of himself at the third ball, spins himself round through (I'll swear) 360 degrees, and in doing so knocks himself flat off the meat of his bat. The Aston players gather over the figure lying by the stumps. A lad dashes out of the pavilion with a bowl of water and a sponge. Consternation ripples round the ground, though a knowing T-shirt suggests "Three pints of lager and he'll be back on his feet." Motherly voices are still anxious when the batsman stands again and indicates his intention to carry

98

on. He gets a great cheer from everybody at this. And another, when he hits the next ball for 4. There is no stopping him after that, as he mows the Aston bowlers all round the little field. This is not a farmer's boy from Tiddington at all: it is another Lord Peter Wimsey who, it will be recalled, was stung by a fast ball on the elbow joint and then proceeded to punish the bowling for the offence.

It is too late to save the game, but it is magnificent while it lasts. One boundary follows another as the sun goes behind evening cloud, and cool air drifts down from the Chiltern ridge, and a wagtail bobs pensively at deep mid-wicket, where no fieldsmen are. If only the boy had gone in higher up the order, Tiddington might have made this a close match. But his first partner, beginning to slog to some effect as well, gets himself bowled, and the last man in soon skies one and is caught. Aston's wicket-keeper thumps triumphantly at the sky again, as the locals cheer their team's victory by 83 runs. But the biggest applause is saved for Tiddington's Number Ten as he strides back, bravely not out for 24, headband damp from his rearguard work above a slightly swollen but still amiable face. "Well done, Geronimo!" someone calls, which enlarges the already seraphic smile. As the players come in, Astonians happily lead a last assault upon the remaining resources of the bar. Tiddington's folk follow them, to quench disappointment before going home. "Ah well," says one philosophically, contemplating the possibilities of the Village Championship's next round. "Ah well, we didn't want to go all the way to Wales – not with all those travelling expenses."

### ASTON ROWANT

| | |
|---|---|
| R. MCQUEEN not out | 107 |
| J. PEARSON c Cross b Wilmshurst | 11 |
| J. HOWELLS b Pykett | 33 |
| W. EDWARDS c Manning b James | 5 |
| P. LAMBOURNE c Robins b Wilmshurst | 3 |
| T. GARRETT b A. Manger | 9 |

| | |
|---|---|
| S. HARDING c and b A. Manger | 2 |
| G. GOLDIE not out | 1 |
| Extras | 6 |
| | |
| Total (for 6, 40 overs) | 177 |

Fall of wickets: 16, 100, 111, 124, 172, 174.

Did not bat: E. Lambourne, M. Jimson, D. Ryan.

Bowling: WILMSHURST 9–2–38–2; A. MANGER 9–4–21–2; ROBINS 3–0–25–0; JAMES 9–0–37–1; PYKETT 9–1–45–1; P. MANGER 1–0–5–0.

## TIDDINGTON

| | |
|---|---|
| W. CROSS c P. Lambourne b E. Lambourne | 9 |
| D. WISE b Garrett | 3 |
| R. MAULE b Goldie | 18 |
| A. MANGER run out | 10 |
| P. MANGER b Goldie | 3 |
| A. COLLINS b Goldie | 2 |
| R. MANNING c Edwards b Goldie | 0 |
| C. WILMSHURST run out | 8 |
| S. ROBINS b Goldie | 11 |
| R. PYKETT not out | 24 |
| P. JAMES c Jimson b Howells | 3 |
| Extras | 3 |
| | |
| Total | 94 |

Fall of wickets: 9, 19, 35, 38, 42, 53, 54, 73, 91

Bowling: GARRETT 5–1–9–0; E. LAMBOURNE 9–2–13–1; RYAN 9–2–27–0; GOLDIE 8–2–21–5; HOWELLS 3.5–1–21–1.

Umpires: P. Salway and I. Smith.

Aston Rowant beat Tiddington by 83 runs.

(In subsequent rounds, they beat Stinchcombe Stragglers, Little Durnford and Ynysygwern. In the semi-final of the championship they were beaten by Linton Park, Kent, who went on to win at Lord's against Toft, from Cheshire.)

# Tourists in the
# West Country

**SOMERSET v NEW ZEALAND**

THERE WAS RAIN IN THE AIR AS WE DROVE ACROSS Sedgemoor after breakfast, but even this grey day cannot spoil my tryst with Taunton. I've had a soft spot for Somerset ever since 1946, when I began watching the first-class game and saw them play Glamorgan during my summer holidays from school. G. R. Langdale hit an unbeaten 69 in less than an hour and everything about Somerset seemed light-hearted and gay, not quite the same cricket I had just become accustomed to at Old Trafford. Thereafter, although Lancashire had first claim to my devotion, the West Country men were held next in succession to my heart. Few days were as sunny as the one on which Maurice Tremlett was cheered from the field at Lord's after his first county match, having taken eight wickets and made the winning hit; until twelve months later, when Harold Gimblett knocked 310 off Sussex for what was then the highest English post-war score. I witnessed neither of these events, but I followed them very closely in print, as I did the doings of the remarkable M. M. Walford, the Sherborne schoolmaster who appeared only in August and scored runs galore, which caused me to weary my mates with the assertion that he was the best batsman who never played for England. Taunton is laden with the memory of men I rarely saw, who made me wistful for their way of playing cricket, even though in match results this produced far fewer ups than downs. I should rejoice in this ground most of all because it was here that Archie MacLaren made his 424 for Lancs in 1895; but the honest truth is that I don't.

Somerset still haven't won a trophy, though this season may change all that. They stand second in the championship this morning, only twelve points behind Kent and going very well, which must be taking years off Horace Hazell and dear old Bertie Buse. It is presumably because they also fancy their chances in the John Player League and the Gillette Cup that they have left so many regulars out of the side today. Botham is away at the last Pakistan Test, but Viv Richards, Burgess, Taylor and Kitchen are also missing from Somerset's ranks, and I can only assume that they are being given a rest during one game that doesn't competitively count. This isn't gracious when the New Zealanders have only just started their tour and could do with all the hard match play they can get before they face the full England side. When Walter Hadlee's team came over in that blazing summer of '49 – which seems, in my memory, to have been dominated by John Arlott's voice describing all aspects of Tom Burtt – Somerset would no more have thought of omitting Gimblett, Lawrence, Wellard and the rest of their backbone from the New Zealand match than of doing so for the Bank Holiday fixture with Gloucestershire. Today's absences have probably made as much difference to the gate as the dour sky which threatens to obscure the Quantocks before the day is out, for the crowd is thin when the captains saunter to the middle, where Brian Rose wins the toss and – in the ancient usage of the Somerset scorecard – "elects" to bat. One omission certainly leaves Somerset a clutch of spectators short. A small boy's head and shoulders appear above the wall on the Coal Orchard side, and he balances there for a moment or two, while he elicits important information from some youngsters who have paid to get in. He transmits this to unseen accomplices waiting outside, then slithers back to join them in search of alternative fun. 'Twasn't worth climbing over when there was no chance of the great Richards batting today.

By the time Rose and Denning make a start, a flurry of drizzle has been and gone, and it is chilly enough for the cricketers to be doubly sweatered, for MacIntyre to protect a bald pate with the black New Zealand cap which appears, these days, to be almost as floppy as the one only Australians used to wear. The batsmen are quick to get their bloodstreams on the move, with Somerset's captain leading the way, Denning more cautious, bending intently as each ball comes on to his bat, as though he wishes to sniff it as well as see it clearly before blocking or striking it away. Rose, immaculately blond and round-shouldered in almost everything he does, drives crisply, playing each shot so that the ball travels close to the grass. The pitch is slow, just as well for anyone batting in this light against Bracewell's pace, which looks pretty brisk. He has a beautiful bowling action, so classically sideways as he spread-eagles himself into his last stride that its logical conclusion should be a gymnastic cartwheel down to the other end. Instead, Bracewell transforms his follow-through into the action of a wild goose landing on water in a rush, body banking right, then left, then right again in rapid succession before coming to a halt.

What on earth, I wonder, does he make of playing cricket in the West of England, which he has never seen before in his life, only eighteen years old, with but three first-class matches behind him before he came on tour? He will perhaps have been disappointed by Taunton as a whole, expecting olde Englyshnesse, finding urbanity instead. But surely some dream will have been fulfilled at the County Ground, where the rustic image does come true, in spite of the lamp standards and other intrusions belonging to the greyhound track? He will not have come across anything as charmingly, as haphazardly cobbled together over a century and more as the pavilion and its attendant stands, where weathered old seats and slender cast-iron posts, narrow passageways and awkward stairs, suggest organic growth through good harvests and bad. That range of building, carpenter's and foundryman's work, is not at all smart like its equivalents at Lord's, Old Trafford or even Canterbury, but its nooks and crannies are as comforting as an old slipper with holes. It is like a covered market in there on match days, full of gossip

about rural things, and you wouldn't be in the least surprised to see men in aprons weighing up bushels from
dusty sacks of corn. There is a way out of this ground
through a garage which looks and smells as if it is where
harrows and seed drills and cultivators are kept, and you
step from it straight into a side street by the church of St
James. While Bracewell bowls this morning, the organist
is practising in there and fragments of Bach and Widor
come drifting over the churchyard wall.

By the time the young New Zealander's first stint is
done, Somerset have reached 40 without much strain.
Dayle Hadlee, replacing him, almost strikes a mortal blow
when he gets Rose plumb on the box, which convulses
some of the fielders with laughter ("Don't rub 'em, count
'em.") and has the batsman on the ground in pain. In
standing order again, Rose drives Hadlee's next ball for 4
and resumes his immaculate strokeplay as before. It is
Denning's wicket that Hadlee takes first, getting one to
flick a bat that has been left hanging in the open. With
only one more run added, Slocombe gets his leg before to
Congdon, the most experienced player in this New Zealand side, and Somerset suddenly look fallible at 64 for
2. The heavy clouds cruising not far above the tower of St
James are helping Congdon's swing, giving him an assistance he can rarely enjoy at home in Christchurch. A man
can bowl for a whole season in the sharp, dry air of Lancaster Park without once losing sight of the Cashmere
Hills through the possibility of rain; but Congdon, on his
fourth English tour, has long since learned how to profit
from damp days like this, when the question is how soon
the Quantocks will vanish and how quickly their disappearance will be followed by a drenching of the County
Ground. With not half the run-up that Bracewell
employed he is producing far more problems for the bat,
getting the ball not only to swing emphatically in flight,
but to cut disagreeably off the pitch. But it is his slowest
delivery so far, the one he holds back, that kids Rose into
a stroke made a fraction too soon, and bowls him on the
verge of half a century.

When lunch comes, Somerset have advanced from 89 to

110 for three and two old university rivals are at the crease. Thirty years ago, I imagine, neither Roebuck (ex-Cambridge) nor Marks (ex-Captain of the other place) would have collected a pay packet for being there. They would have inserted themselves somewhere in that endless procession of Somerset amateurs who popped in and out of the side and kept my adolescent eyes fairly blinking at their great wealth of initials – G. E. S. Woodhouse, R. J. O. Meyer, C. J. P. Barnwell, A. T. M. Jones and all the rest (ah, how I could rattle every one of them off in the Upper Fourth). Lunch reveals another tradition that has gone by the board, when I ask for a pint of draught cider in the refreshment shed and am told that the stuff comes only in bottles now. Maybe Roebuck and Marks have had access to genuine scrumpy in the players' den, for when they carry on after the break their batting has a fluency that was missing from their morning play. Then they seemed nervously aware of a need to guard their wickets and save their side from more harm. Now they begin to attack with confidence and Marks is quite the more belligerent of the two, springing youth eagerly brandishing his bat. The taller Roebuck bats with more dignity, studying each delivery with a dispassionate air before deciding what judgment to pass upon it with which stroke. I am not just accommodating this description to a knowledge that Roebuck read law at Cambridge (though, fancifully, I reckon that thin, bespectacled face has been bred to anticipate a full-bottomed wig even more than a county cap). A man's temperament shows on a cricket field, and when he has chosen law as an ultimate career he cultivates gravity even when his instincts may be those of a buccaneer. Just after lunch Roebuck drives Congdon to the boundaries off successive balls. The second of these shots finds him erect and slim as it is delivered; then he bobs down, bending both knees quickly, and hits the ball impeccably straight past the bowler to the ropes. The movement is neat, not gaudy, the effect disproportionate to the absolute control exercised in the blow.

New Zealand are handicapped by the breakdown of Hadlee, who spends his afternoon on a physiotherapist's couch, having treatment for a troublesome back. A jinx seems to have struck widely during lunch. Howarth goes sick and Taunton's decrepit public address system tells us he will play no further part in the match, that Wright will take his place on the tourists' side. Somerset's Gurr also falls out, and Taylor is recalled from his three-day leave. One way and another, this fixture is becoming a game of musical chairs, and the spectators who stayed away to watch Wimbledon and the Third Test on TV may think they have chosen well. By mid-afternoon this is still a miserable crowd for a touring match, not enough to muster the cheers that the batting of Roebuck and Marks begins to merit. It produces a substantial groan, though, when the partnership is stupidly dissolved. Roebuck strikes Congdon past mid-on and decides there isn't time for an elegant run. Marks, unfortunately, thinks there's all the time in the world; as, indeed, there is if only his partner will move. He rushes right down to the other end and is halfway back again before his wicket is broken, what time Roebuck has stood perfectly still in his ground with an air that suggests he is baffled by the sudden appearance of a lunatic scampering up and down the pitch. Marks deserved better than that and his run-out is a shame. It also causes Roebuck to retreat into private gloom for a while. Four more runs are added and three of them are scored by the newcomer, Olive, who then tries to cut another ball and gets himself caught in the slips.

Roebuck is thus joined, at 162 for 5, by the jaunty figure of Breakwell, who wanders out in flannels that look as if they just happened to be lying around, complete with pink stains fore and aft from much polishing of the ball. This careless approach doubtless accounts for some of the applause that accompanies his going to the crease; but the warmth that follows Breakwell from the members' enclosure has also been generated by that twinkle in his eye, by that jester's always lurking grin. He is the sort of cricketer who makes crowds pleased they have turned up on the dullest day, even when he is having little effect on a match. This afternoon he will transform it so much that we shall barely be conscious of large rain drops that sometimes fall from the clouds. He begins to hit from the moment he arrives and at first we settle indulgently for a quick and merry knock that may yield Breakwell twenty-odd runs before he miscalculates and is caught somewhere in the deep. Somerset supporters have been well used to batting like that for donkey's years and it's all right by them so long as something respectable is already on the board. But as Breakwell bounds into the thirties with not much more than half an hour gone, we decide there is no telling what he might achieve today. A handful of youngsters who have been playing a game of their own at the river end ever since lunch, pause more often to watch Breakwell's progress, finally lay down their arms and surrender to the sight. He is not simply slogging the New Zealand bowlers round the ground; he is distinguishing very finely between the good balls and the loose ones, and playing some instructive strokes of pure defence. On this nebulous day at Taunton, Breakwell's eye is clear and bright. Just once he shapes a massive cover drive off Thomson and, barely touching it with the butt of his bat, sees the ball swerve dizzily in an arc round slips. He up-ends the bat to examine the butt, smiles happily at the infielders, cocks his head matily at the laughter from the crowd.

With such companionship out there, Roebuck gradually comes out of exile, reaches his half century and begins to pick up Breakwell's rhythm in attack. As he sees Somerset's innings mount, Burgess turns to MacIntyre's spin in an effort to restrain these two. MacIntyre is a busy, restless bowler, forever hitching his flannels, wiping his nose or his bald forehead on his sweater sleeve, every child's sporting uncle bouncing near the centre of all play. He flights some balls cunningly enough to have the batsmen going quite extravagantly the wrong way. Roebuck takes four quick steps down the wicket to one delivery, bat swinging to drive it into the stand, then suddenly stoops, stifling his shot and smothering the ball at the pitch instead. Mostly, though, MacIntyre is punished like everybody else but Congdon, in whom all the virtues of the mythical New Zealander seem to reside – not as

107

aggressive as the congenital Australian or half as loud, but self-contained, worthy and not given to flap. Congdon slouches away from the ends of his overs without emotion even when he has been hit for a couple of 4s, phlegmatic man with resilience in his blood. He could do with a much better fielding side than this one to back him, though. Some of these Kiwis are awfully slow to bend and pick up. Roebuck and Breakwell run 4 because deep third man cannot nearly reach the wicketkeeper with his throw, causing Edwards to charge, pads slopping, a good fifteen yards to collect the ball.

As these two batsmen surge past tea, the years fall away and I can see another partnership that would pillage bowling like this to make Somerset look briefly the most exciting team in the land. M. M. Walford and Arthur Wellard were just such a pair, the one cultured and classical in every stroke he made, the other picked for his bowling but a magnificent hitter on his day. One corner of the County Ground is bordered by a high white wooden wall, which helps to make Taunton such a cosy cricketing place. Wellard used to hit balls over the top, into the river beyond, whereas Walford's way was to make the base of the wall shudder and crack. Something of the same distinction is there between Roebuck and Breakwell now, as the slender young man races for his century, with the twinkling jester hard on his heels. Roebuck does not put many balls in the air, any more than Walford did, and when Breakwell does hit them through the sky he has by instinct and management aimed them towards an empty patch of the field. Hadlee, who has returned after tea, supplies Roebuck with his hundred as soon as he takes over from the battered Bracewell, with the batsman on 98. His first ball is pulled to mid-wicket for 4, his second smacked past the square leg umpire and into the seats in one bounce. After the first of these shots, with applause for the century pattering round the ground, Roebuck raises his cap delicately, in the old-fashioned way. R. J. O. Meyer probably insisted on that, when Roebuck was one of his pupils at Millfield School.

With the Somerset score approaching 300, the only

uncertainty is whether Breakwell will also get a century, the first of his long career, before a declaration comes. He slows up a bit as he nears the nineties, conscious of demons that have frustrated him hereabouts before. He is still grinning happily at every encouragement from the crowd but he is tense now as he addresses each ball, concentrating on technique which earlier was allowed to take care of itself. He settles for stylish singles, the occasional elaborate 2, while Roebuck goes galloping on to his own highest score. Burgess brings in Bracewell again, hoping that a quick change will disturb Breakwell the more. But the bowler overpitches, offering Breakwell meat and drink. He leaps and drives a mighty 6 straight past the bowler with such force that, as the ball hits the stand at the river end, an advertisement for The County Warehouse is dislodged and falls to the ground with a thump. Now the youngsters are yelling down there and, in the members' enclosure, gentleman farmers are slapping the benches and bellowing as though Breakwell were a favourite hound. He does not disappoint them, but throws his last caution to the wind and gets that century with a cross-batted swipe and a palpitating run. At once Brian Rose calls his men in. Roebuck walks back with the same composure that I think he would have maintained if he'd been out for a duck. Breakwell strides towards the pavilion blissfully, moustache curled mockingly at the demons, cheerfulness splitting his face. Together they have made 187 in a couple of hours, and Breakwell's share has included two 6s and fourteen 4s.

Walford and Wellard could have done no more. Nor could Harold Gimblett, greatest Somerset batsman of them all, whose famous first innings at Frome must in character have been a bit like Breakwell's today. He should have been alive to see this season, when his team might at last triumph in a way it never managed to when he was its chief prop and stay; but he went in March, another in that extraordinary, hauntingly long line of cricketers who have taken life and death in their own hands. As the New Zealand openers carefully gather 25 runs in the day's last half hour, and Dennis Breakwell at third man glances with satisfaction at the hoarding he broke in two, it is Gimblett's memory that stirs me in Taunton's twilight grey. He persevered, often fruitlessly, in this game of cricket with this one unsuccessful county club, and never thought to sell himself elsewhere to a prizewinning team. He gladdened my youth and made me wish that I could play like him, vividly, sturdily, but gallantly above all.

## SOMERSET — *First Innings*

| | |
|---|---:|
| B. C. ROSE b Congdon | 49 |
| P. W. DENNING c Edwards b Hadlee | 24 |
| P. A. SLOCOMBE lbw Congdon | 1 |
| P. M. ROEBUCK not out | 131 |
| V. J. MARKS run out | 23 |
| M. OLIVE c Congdon b Bracewell | 3 |
| D. BREAKWELL not out | 100 |
| Extras (b 4, lb 11, nb 3) | 18 |
| Total (for 5, declared) | 349 |

Fall of wickets: 63, 64, 89, 158, 162.

Did not bat: K. Jennings, C. Dredge, D. J. S. Taylor, T. Gard.

Bowling: BRACEWELL 19–2–80–1; THOMSON 17–3–63–0; HADLEE 16–0–70–1; CONGDON 22–5–50–2; MACINTYRE 18–3–68–0.

## *Second Innings*

| | |
|---|---:|
| P. W. DENNING c Congdon b MacIntyre | 38 |
| M. OLIVE lbw Bracewell | 1 |
| P. A. SLOCOMBE b Thomson | 8 |
| V. J. MARKS b MacIntyre | 31 |
| D. J. S. TAYLOR c Anderson b Congdon | 11 |
| P. M. ROEBUCK not out | 23 |
| B. C. ROSE c Burgess b MacIntyre | 16 |
| D. BREAKWELL not out | 4 |
| Extras (lb 2, nb 2) | 4 |
| Total (for 6, declared) | 144 |

Fall of wickets: 4, 34, 77, 86, 94, 119.

Bowling: BRACEWELL 80–0–19–1; THOMSON 10–3–34–1; CONGDON 20–5–47–1; MACINTYRE 17–6–40–3.

## NEW ZEALAND—*First Innings*

| | |
|---|---|
| R. W. ANDERSON c Denning b Breakwell | 40 |
| B. A. EDGAR c Gard b Breakwell | 81 |
| J. M. PARKER c Slocombe b Breakwell | 5 |
| M. G. BURGESS run out | 0 |
| B. E. CONGDON b Marks | 38 |
| J. G. WRIGHT b Dredge | 13 |
| G. N. EDWARDS c Rose b Jennings | 25 |
| D. R. HADLEE b Jennings | 8 |
| J. M. MACINTYRE not out | 2 |
| B. P. BRACEWELL not out | 0 |
| Extras (b 4, lb 2) | 6 |
| | |
| Total (for 8 declared) | 218 |

Fall of wickets: 66, 83, 87, 170, 176, 208, 208, 218.
Did not bat: G. B. Thomson
Bowling: DREDGE 15–3–29–1; JENNINGS 15–4–30–2; MARKS 31–10–71–1; BREAKWELL 31–7–64–3; ROSE 2–0–10–0; ROEBUCK 1–0–3–0.

## Second Innings

| | |
|---|---|
| R. W. ANDERSON not out | 37 |
| B. A. EDGAR not out | 54 |
| Extras (lb 1, w 1) | 2 |
| | |
| Total (for 0) | 93 |

Bowling: DREDGE 9–0–31–0; JENNINGS 5–1–18–0; BREAKWELL 12–4–22–0; MARKS 8–2–20–0.
Umpires: D. Evans and B. Meyer.
Match drawn.

# The Oldest Fixture

*July 15*                                                      *Lord's*

## ETON v HARROW

THE SCHOOLBOYS PICKED A PERFECT DAY FOR THE START of the annual ceremony at Lord's. Cricket was meant to be enjoyed under just such a cloudless sky, with players, watchers and everything about the ground glowing with midsummer warmth. This, at any rate, is how imagination persists in idealising the game, misinforming us that rain never stopped play in the traditional past. And here, at the Eton and Harrow match, we are at the deep end of cricketing tradition, for this fixture has a longer history than any other cricket match still being played. The schools probably met in 1804, certainly in the following year, when lame young Lord Byron scored 7 and 2 for Harrow with the assistance of a runner, and afterwards conceded that they had been "most confoundedly beat" by Eton. Early records of the rivalry are incomplete, but from 1822 onwards the two sides have turned out at Lord's each year almost without a break apart from the interruptions of war. The University match didn't get under way until 1827, organised county and international cricket were even further behind. A man comes to the Eton and Harrow, therefore, with a healthy regard for seniority, even if he has no commitment to any of these downy lads.

He should also, of course, bring a taste for social history if he is to savour the day to the full. When the Eton openers begin to bat this morning, and the zebra caps of Harrow stripe the infield grass, there will be nobody on this ground unconscious of the fact that he is attending an occasion for which the cricket itself is not much more than the excuse. To some extent this is true of all cricket matches, where wider loyalties are invariably at stake, but the Eton and Harrow crowd make this a particularly arresting example of tribal display. Devotion to the schools has brought them here, as well as pride in siblings and sons, but the majority, I think, are attracted to Lord's for these two days in every year to exhibit a more substantial *esprit de corps*. During the first half hour's play, when Compton-Burnett and Morris are struggling to master some steady bowling from the Harrow attack, there is much more clapping out on the pitch, from players who have been drilled in the politenesses of this game, than there is from the spectators, who are still settling down to their own performances of the day. Nine-tenths of them are congregated by the Tavern, or in immediately adjacent seats, and this will not just be because the wicket for this match is closer to that side. It is as much an expression of solidarity as any gathering of strikers outside a factory gate. This is, for the most part, the assembly of an elite whom history has been overhauling this past forty years. There is comfort in whatever numbers remain.

Neither the numbers nor anything else about this fixture are what they were when George du Maurier caricatured the spectators as a languid lot with impedimented speech. At the end of the nineteenth century, and for many years after, stagecoaches were driven to Lord's and encircled the field this day, so that ladies and gentlemen could watch the affair from some height and in much elegance. Today, a solitary vehicle in yellow and brown has been parked by the covers at the Nursery end, lonely memorial to a gracious past, with five people sitting on tubular deckchairs in its lee. Grey toppers and morning suits are still just holding their own, propped up, here and there, by an ivory-handled stick. The Harrovian quota is distinguishable by that suburban annual in the lapel, and the proportion of cornflowers at Lord's today suggests that Eton face overwhelming odds in support. "This is supposed to be the strongest Eton batting side for years, isn't it?" enquires one such gentleman of another on a Tavern bench. It doesn't look like it, when Feather and Murray replace the opening bowlers and Eton wickets begin to go down. By the time Feather takes

Benthall's off-stump out of the ground, the Etonians have mustered only 37 for 3. At this point, sheets of pale Cambridge blue are hung in front of two boxes on the Tavern stand, to match the colour of the Eton caps. They look like frayed washing but they are meant to rally a cause.

And in those boxes above the Tavern bar, the quintessential spectators of the Eton and Harrow match are themselves to be seen. There are similar boxes on the Grandstand side of the ground, similarly filled with people who must be straining their eyes to observe details of the play; though, as I say, they have posted themselves there for reasons other than that. These boxes have been hired for princely sums by Mr E. W. Swanton, Mr C. Martin-Jenkins, Brigadier Gordon Lennox and their peers for the purpose of entertaining guests, which they appear to do handsomely and well, judging by the parade of Bloody Marys and other intoxicants visible through the rails. Blander visions carefully stay within view, decked in fashions scarcely seen nowadays outside Ascot and garden parties at the Palace. A woman poises herself at one balcony above the Tavern, exquisitely modelled in white; dress flowing from chin to floor, hat brimming widely beyond her head, ribbons fluttering down her back, the whiteness relieved only by a small cameo in china at her throat. When Dudley Carew wrote his short story about the Eton and Harrow match some time after the Great War, he portrayed a Gainsborough lady who intently followed every incident of play, motionless on a bench down there on the grass. Her counterpart today leans conversationally on the rail above, toying with a gin and tonic, early Anna Neagle in a production by Herbert Wilcox.

Wickets continue to fall in quick time, until Eton have descended to 42 for 6 and Harrow's slip fielders are crouched behind the batsman as tight-strung as any arc of professionals scenting victory in a Test. Batsmen come out with determination in their walk, to return shortly afterwards more slowly, with cap shoved back and a puzzled expression on the face. There will be some very old Etonians who must already be bracing themselves on the memory of Fowler's match in 1910, whose outcome sensationally reversed the general pattern of play. Eton followed-on 165 behind that year, and were only 4 runs ahead when the ninth wicket of their second innings fell. They won by 9 runs largely because R. St L. Fowler, who had made Eton's top score twice, bowled ten overs of off-breaks that took 8 Harrovians for only 23. For the moment, the people wearing cornflowers are enjoying much the better of things, and this corner of Lord's becomes raucous with a peculiar cry of triumph and joy. It is a prolonged version of the school's name, rendered full-throated as "Harr-oho! Harr-oho!" Gentlemen in top hats are shouting it, as well as Harrow boys, necks straining upwards to throw the cry out, so that it looks as well as sounds like the baying of hounds. But it would be misleading to imply that these are the only origins of the Harrow cry. There are two strangers in that Tavern crowd, standing by the benches that border the fence. They flourish no cornflowers, are not smartly dressed, men of indeterminate age whose eyes never leave the cricket except when one or other of them goes to fetch pints for them both. One has a silk scarf tucked into his shirt, and a bushy moustache, image of a Spitfire pilot during the war. The other's face is keen and tanned, suggesting regimental duty in some burnished land. They mutter to each other, words that do not always properly form, and the Spitfire pilot giggles mirthlessly whenever an Eton player misses his shot. The other catches my eye and grins with a friendly nod. "Oh, they're doin' very well today, aren't they? Very well indeed!" Then he joins his companion in the Harrow cry, to which they add embellishments of their own. "Let's 'ave another one, Harr-ohoho! Give 'em the 'ammer, Harr-ohoho!" They do not bay like hounds, those two. They croon the words gently, as parents lull infants to sleep.

Davies and Speke mount a rearguard action, which quietens some of the Harrow noise and brings Eton to lunch with 64 runs and no further loss. Large hampers are opened here and there around the Tavern seats, revealing contents that would satisfy appetites and thirsts at

Glyndebourne just as well. Up in the boxes even greater
gastronomic feats have been prepared while, down at the
stagecoach, the boot below the whip's seat has been
opened to disclose a cocktail cabinet as well stocked as
any that ever fortified a boardroom. Yet, although a
decade or more has passed since every Eton schoolboy
was obliged to turn up at this match, there are still enough
youths without parents on the ground to make inroads
into the heaps of sausage rolls and meat pies that are forever the stand-by at Lord's. The lads are having a terrible
time trying to extract beer from the bar, though, with the
caterers insisting on proof that dubious customers are
over eighteen. I suspect that some of the top hats were
not, in their day, so bound to abide by the law. One
lunch-time habit has certainly suffered a change. It was a
tradition of the Eton and Harrow match that all its elegance, all this finery of toppers and tulle, should take to
the field at the break and stroll for mutual admiration on
pretext of examining the pitch. Today the field stays
empty until a dozen people set off for the middle just
before the umpires reappear, and five of them are
children in jeans.

Many of the schoolboys watching this game are similarly clad; not one Eton collar is anywhere in sight. But the
most extraordinary thing about these supporting youths,
a highly conversational group, is that their talk does not
refer to this or to any other cricket match. As Eton begin to
bat again, judgment is deilvered on an absent competitor
in another field. "He finally got an exhibition to Cambridge – sickening creep!" Speke drives Lloyd-Jones
through the covers for 4, inspiring a young spectator to
turn to a friend with a sudden thought. "What profits did
your father's firm make last year?" he asks. A very new
old boy is hailed by some fellows with incredulity border-
ing on surprise. "Don't say you work at Coutts as well?"
and there are moments, listening to the babble along the
Tavern seats, when one forms the impression that without Harrow the merchant banking system might be distinctly different in tone. When they do address themselves to their team, the young Harrovians are not always

kind. Sealey flings himself sideways to catch Davies marvellously in the slips, and mid-wicket, standing very
deep, looks pleased that this obstruction has been
removed. "Don't smile, Edward," calls one of his chums
from the crowd, "It spoils the makeup." Surnames
evidently went out of public school life along with flog-
ging and fags.

The two strangers are still rapt, still crooning their alle-
giance to Winston Churchill's old school. "Get 'em on the
run again, Harr-ohoho! Let's 'ave another wicket,
Harr-ohoho!" They are missing nothing out there as Eton
go into final collapse. Someone else watches steadily from
the crowd in front of the Tavern bar, a tall and heavy man,
red-faced these days, with much grey in his thickly swept
hair and fine veins running along a predator's nose.
Cardus once wrote of this spectator that "his attitude to
cricket is almost as obsolete as chivalry": after his last
match here, with ten wickets under his belt, he tossed the
bails into the MCC members' seats, a gesture as lordly as
any man could make. But that was twenty-two years ago,
and I see no hint that anyone by the Tavern has recog-
nised Keith Miller today. There is first-class cricket at the
Oval this afternoon but the incomparable Miller, of
Melbourne, New South Wales and Australia, has chosen
to be at Lord's, to watch a bunch of schoolboys play.
Perhaps, like the besotted racegoer he has always been,
he wishes to spot promising youngsters before they are
entered for major events. In this case it will be a hopeful
quest more than a reasonable bet, for the plain fact is that
neither Eton nor Harrow has produced an England
cricketer for even longer than Miller has been out of the
game, not since F. G. Mann (of Eton) captained the side
against New Zealand in 1949. These boys play with great
style, though their coaching now seems to permit certain
departures from the classical rules; young Morris this
morning faced the bowling like Mike Brearley, standing
upright with bat hanging a foot off the ground. This may
or may not be one reason why the Eton and Harrow
match no longer deserves the reputation it once had,
when it fostered great cricketing talents like those of F. S.

Jackson and the ineffable Lord Hawke. It is not merely the trappings that have been reduced over the years. Wisden still logs the match attentively, because of its place in the history of the game, but the *Telegraph* newspapers are now the only ones that give the scores in full. Keith Miller is an accolade of which these boys should be proud, and it would be nice to record that some of them rush up to him with scorecards to be signed as he stands there with his pint, old devil-may-care himself, giant in a sloppy cardigan with its buttons undone. But nobody does.

Speke is still there when Eton struggle to 100 for 9, still not out when they are dismissed for 112. Without his 30 runs they would have made a very sorry show and, though they quickly take Sealey's wicket when Harrow come to bat, it is not long before they are thrust on the defensive again. For that exuberant moment when Harrow are 1 for 1, the outnumbered Etonians in the crowd raise a lusty counter-cheer, and it is the first time today they have really made their presence heard. Presently their noise subsides, as Wiggin gets the measure of the attack and starts to collect runs. Even more so does Haggas, a self-possessed young man who struts round his wicket like a turkey cock when he is not cutting deliciously and driving balls to the off with wristy strokes. This pair take Harrow up to 69 by tea and, as the fieldsmen of Eton clap them off, their ears ring to the triumphant baying of their crowd. The Harrovian din, indeed, has been unabated since they began to score, and only the ladies seem to have exempted themselves from contributing to the noise. Among these is a formidable matron, gloved to the elbows and cultured with pearl, whose conversation since that wicket fell has steadily perambulated through her acquaintance with Sir John Betjeman, Virginia Wade and a gentleman who owns a flamingo park. The decorum of Lord's, so much extolled by historians of the game and to be expected, perhaps, at this fixture above all, only descends when the gladiators are out of sight. Two grey toppers pause conspiratorially in the alley behind the stands, one watching closely the other's face, which scrutinises the asphalt and the ferrule of an ebony stick, and otherwise offers advice full of portent through rather tight lips. There may be a killing on Monday, when the City gets going.

There is no stopping Harrow after tea, as Wiggin and Haggas belabour the bowling again, exceeding Eton's total by themselves before another wicket falls. Then Harrow's captain, James, comes out and continues where Wiggin left off, and it is clear that unless Eton can produce another Fowler from the back of their hand, they are not going to win the 143rd contest between the sides. In the golden light of midsummer, as an evening sun still burns warmly above the pavilion at Lord's, all this is a remembrancer of cricket's Golden Age. Young men, mere boys with sharp and eager limbs, are bending themselves to the game as though nothing in the world mattered but this, then wandering across the field slowly, having been taught that it is well to be casual about even the most momentous things. Some of the watchers have been nurtured to treat the whole of life like that, while others are still acquiring the habit, for it is not a thing that can be instantly bought. Thus the Eton and Harrow is balanced betwixt and between, with graceful combat on the cricket field, with the pandemonium of conquest coming from its edge. And with those two strangers, who have been watchful all day, still murmuring their chant in a long lost undertone. "Let's 'ave some more, Harr-ohoho! Keep the pot boilin', Harr-ohoho! Give 'em the 'ammer, Harr-ohoho!"

ETON—*First Innings*

| | | |
|---|---|---|
| R. J. COMPTON-BURNETT c Jackson b Feather | | 12 |
| P. W. MORRIS lbw Murray | | 9 |
| P. J. R. GOULDER c James b Feather | | 9 |
| C. H. BENTHALL b Feather | | 0 |
| J. R. BOUGHEY b Murray | | 2 |
| P. D. WHITBY b Feather | | 2 |
| C. J. DAVIES c Sealey b James | | 27 |

| | |
|---|---:|
| C. C. SPEKE not out | 30 |
| C. G. CRACE b James | 0 |
| J. R. C. MCLEOD b James | 0 |
| P. J. N. BARKER b Lloyd-Jones | 5 |
| Extras (b 2, lb 3, w 5, nb 6) | 16 |
| | |
| Total | 112 |

Fall of wickets: 24, 32, 37, 40, 40, 42, 89, 100, 100.

Bowling: LLOYD-JONES 11–4–13–1; JAMES 20–9–32–3; FEATHER 15–4–35–4; MURRAY 14–5–12–2; HAGGAS 3–0–4–0.

## Second Innings

| | |
|---|---:|
| R. J. COMPTON-BURNETT lbw James | 0 |
| P. J. R. GOULDER run out | 59 |
| P. W. MORRIS hit wicket b Murray | 26 |
| C. H. BENTHALL run out | 3 |
| J. R. BOUGHEY c Ruffell b Murray | 73 |
| P. D. WHITBY b Murray | 7 |
| C. J. DAVIES c Sealey b Haggas | 9 |
| C. C. SPEKE b Lloyd-Jones | 1 |
| C. G. CRACE lbw James | 0 |
| J. R. C. MCLEOD not out | 0 |
| P. J. N. BARKER not out | 0 |
| Extras (b 15, lb 9, nb 13, w 4) | 41 |
| | |
| Total (for 9) | 219 |

Fall of wickets: 8, 37, 43, 170, 179, 197, 203, 212, 219.

Bowling: LLOYD-JONES 16–10–18–1; JAMES 20–9–46–2; HAGGAS 8–3–11–1; FEATHER 11–1–41–0; MURRAY 21–8–39–3; SEALEY 9–3–23–0.

## HARROW—First Innings

| | |
|---|---:|
| D. P. WIGGIN b Crace | 41 |
| M. L. SEALEY b McLeod | 0 |
| W. J. HAGGAS c Boughey b Crace | 65 |
| T. M. H. JAMES not out | 112 |
| T. R. JACKSON c Compton-Burnett b Davies | 21 |

| | |
|---|---|
| E. C. GORDON LENNOX b Crace | 47 |
| M. W. J. RUFFELL st Whitby b Barker | 34 |
| J. F. P. LLOYD-JONES not out | 2 |
| Extras (b 11, lb 7, w 1) | 19 |
| | |
| Total (for 6 declared) | 341 |

Fall of wickets: 1, 116, 121, 165, 261, 336.

Did not bat: C. L. Feather, A. R. G. Murray, W. N. G. Taylor.

Bowling: MCLEOD 12–3–42–1; DAVIES 22–4–87–1; CRACE 32–6–75–3; BENTHALL 1–0–10–0; BARKER 24–8–89–1; SPEKE 4–1–18–0.

Umpires: A. Edmondson and H. E. Robinson.

Match drawn.

# Minor Counties

## STAFFORDSHIRE v NORTHUMBERLAND

IT TOOK HALF AN HOUR THIS MORNING TO FIND ANYONE
who could tell us where their county cricketers were playing. The game began yesterday, but it might not be
happening for all most of the locals seem to know or care.
The match should be an event in their sporting life when
Staffordshire so rarely make an appearance here, these
players circumnavigating their county almost as much as
do those of Essex and Kent. By the time we arrive at the
ground of Lichfield CC, Staffs have gone just ahead of
Northumberland's first innings score of 196 for 7 and have
then declared in their turn. All is to play for on this remaining day, with only a couple of runs separating the
sides, and a warm breeze keeps puffballs of cloud moving
across a sunny sky. Yet I doubt whether twenty people
have turned up to watch the game on this edge of the little
town, whose cathedral spires prick the middle distance
above the pavilion roof.

I suspect this is a common experience for minor county
teams, which occupy a curiously ambiguous position in
the pattern of English cricket. They are not regarded as
intrinsically first-class by the legislators of the game but
they are allowed occasional combat with first-class sides,
which they sometimes defeat, as Durham did Yorkshire in
1973, as Hertfordshire did Essex in 1976. Though they
would resist any suggestion that they partly exist for the
convenience of first-class county clubs, the minor counties
championship has usually included some first-class
Second XIs, whose players are either maturing or de-
moted out of form. There has always been a process of
graduation from the minor to the major county game and,
although in this century only Northamptonshire and

Glamorgan have achieved it as clubs, it has been common for individuals to make the move. Four members of the Edrich clan played for Norfolk before they made their names with first-class sides, Peter May was introduced to county cricket in Berkshire, not Surrey, and an adolescent David Steele played several seasons for his home county here in Staffs. Performing mostly as amateurs, the minor counties men are at the same time organised in a professional way on the outskirts of the professional game. When cricket watchers had to consider bus timetables much more than they nowadays do, the minor county teams reaped a partisan reward. The motorised age has damaged local loyalty at this level perhaps more than at any other, vastly increasing the temptation to visit the nearest first-class ground instead and watch a county match decorated with international stars.

Before a bare quorum of watchers, then, Staffordshire strike quickly when Northumberland's second innings begins. Youll is run out before anything has been scored and a second wicket is taken before 20 runs have been notched. Younger and Craig move very cautiously after this for some time and turn the morning into an excessively laborious affair, as they steadily block most of what is coming their way. They take runs only when absolutely confident they can make their ground. Once in a while the ball is struck to the edge of the field and a fieldsman has to turn and pursue. On one boundary this means that he appears from a distance to be gradually sinking into the turf up to his chest, for this is not a level cricket ground; it dips and curves on the perimeter like a warped old gramophone record. Silently the handful of spectators watch these concentrated movements about the field; almost silently the game of cricket drifts towards 69 for two at lunch. What noise there is usually comes from Staffordshire's wicketkeeper, Green, who shouts and flings his arms up now and then, possibly to reduce the chances of petrifying where he is. Otherwise he is a squat figure, made more so by the way he wears his cap, with its peak turned up to admit more light. He is wearing it in pride, not to shade his eyes from the sun.

Shortly after lunch the crowd is instantly doubled, possibly more than that, when a schoolmaster leads a class of children through the gate. They sprawl attentively along the mid-wicket grass, and I hope the teacher is managing to convey the keeper's pride in that green county cap with the golden Staffordshire knot for a badge. It is, after all, one of the most famous of all cricket emblems, though that is not because Staffs have always been one of the leading minor county sides, winning the championship as often as anyone except Buckinghamshire, their own record matched only by Durham and the Lancashire Second XI. That cap has been familiar to generations who have never seen Staffordshire play, through paintings and photographs and the tab cards once purveyed by W. D. & H. O. Wills, because for twenty-three seasons it was worn by S. F. Barnes. Can that teacher, I wonder, possibly make those children realise the colossal, the unique accomplishment of Sydney Barnes? Even more difficult, the deeply rooted character of the man? He can tell them that it is still the opinion of sages that Barnes was the greatest bowler who ever lived, a man who could produce genuine spin bowling at medium pace and more; who once dismissed Trumper with a ball that was delivered fast on the leg stump, swung to the off before it pitched, then broke back and took the leg-stump out of the ground. ("The sort of ball," said Charlie Macartney, who watched it from the non-striker's crease, "a man might see if he was dreaming or drunk.") The teacher can also review the remarkable statistics of Barnes's career – the 189 Test wickets at 16.43 apiece in only twenty-seven games, the 1,432 wickets for Staffordshire that cost no more than 8 runs each – and he can point out that Barnes is still the only man ever picked for England while playing minor county and league cricket. But how does he suggest the toughness and the unbending self-assurance of Sydney Barnes, who knew his own worth and demanded that it be paid, who deliberately let Jessop slog him round Old Trafford one day to spite Archie MacLaren, who had insisted on setting what Barnes thought an unacceptable field?

Sydney Barnes spent so long with Staffordshire, so little time with first-class teams, because the Establishment of the day was not prepared to bend itself to him. He would, of course, have given Mr Packer's organisation a trial had he been playing now, though I suspect the association might not have lasted long, tycoons being generally less willing than lordlings to let gifted eccentrics go their own way. I hope, above all, the teacher points out something else about S. F. Barnes. He was still bowling for Staffordshire, on his native heath, when he was sixty-one years old. I do not think such identity, such enthusiasm or such endurance will be within reach of the Ian Chappells and the Tony Greigs.

By the time those children arrive, the cricket's tempo has increased from *adagio* to *andante*, perhaps because the Northumbrians have noted the lateness of the hour and because Staffs have introduced spin bowling of something less than medium pace. There is rather more work for the fieldsmen now, as both batsmen begin to chance their arms. When Younger lifts Nasim into rosebay willowherb by the wall flanking the Birmingham road, the children plunge like terriers into the undergrowth to find the ball. Presently the century is hoisted on Lichfield's rudimentary board. This causes Hancock to make a bowling change, and he brings in a man with another name that rings. I never saw his father play for Staffordshire, either at the start of his county career or at its close, but I used to watch him during his Lancashire heyday in between, the finest slip catcher of his generation and good enough in other respects to play eighteen times for England and tour Australia with Hammond's team. Jack Ikin's phlegmatic spin bowling was often expensive, but had the knack of quickly breaking partnerships that had gone on too long. Black hair flowing as he bounds towards the crease, Michael Ikin now performs the same service for Staffs with medium pace. Younger is lbw to the very first ball and Northumberland are 101 for 3.

The afternoon is largely placid, though, the visitors evidently trying to construct the makings of a respectable draw. After lunch it takes them 135 minutes to accumulate

100 runs on a wicket that wouldn't induce a golf ball to bounce. They lose two more batsmen in that time and, when each of these goes, the Staffordshire players loll on the grass while they await the new man. They will tell themselves, I imagine, that they are conserving their energies for tomorrow, when they meet Sussex in the Gillette Cup at Stone, though their relaxation seems much more consistent with a lack of challenge in the air today. It is not that they are behaving sluggishly when they are on their feet, merely that they are adjusting to an atmosphere when they have a chance. They are keeping this match tight, which is no more than you would expect of cricketers bred round here. Most of the Staffordshire images, after all, are tenacious ones; bull terriers and knots, Black Country locks and chains; even Staffordshire's most delicate pottery originated in a landscape so hellish that the first instinct of inhabitants must always have been to hang on. There is another side to the county, though, and it is represented here on the Lichfield ground. At one end of the pitch stands the sightscreen by En-Tout-Cas in front of trees, at the other is nothing but a vision of cornfields gently sloping down and then up a roll in the land. The harder side of Staffordshire makes only a token show here, in that long terrace of workers' cottages, two-up and two-down, that faces the cricket ground on the other side of the Birmingham road, beyond the low stone wall. A factory stands behind the terrace, then nothing but more fields. If the cricket has been peaceful so far, it has come to terms with a prevailing mood in the surrounding district.

Even the elders of Northumberland are affected by it, as their team proceeds temperately to teatime and beyond. Three or four members of the committee have come half-way across England to father their lads (in a manner of speaking, with two grey heads playing for the side), full of counsel that may come in handy if the captain finds himself stuck for strategy or ploy. It is doubtless they who have transported the big Northumbrian shield, with its red and gold stripes, that is propped up against the pavilion wall. This morning those committee men were keeping their counsel on the benches inside the pavilion's fence; later, one of them stood on the opposite boundary, talking cricket with one of the team. Now the old men and a couple of wives are sitting like roadside picnickers, on deckchairs by their cars in another corner of the ground, listening to one of their number hold forth in bass Geordie tones about some work he's having done by a builder at home. A couple of them speculate about the purpose of the factory behind the terrace over there. "Have you been and got your strawberries yet, then?" one asks another, nodding towards the farm across the boundary ditch, where fruit is to be had for 25p a punnet if you go and pick it yourself. Between them, the elders keep an eye on the cricket, but not much more than that. It has become that sort of game.

At a quarter to five, Northumberland at last declare with 181 for 5 and, as Staffordshire's innings starts, a few more people begin to dribble in through the gate. The home side need 180 to win and they have ninety-five minutes plus 20 overs in which to get the runs, which will require a rate of scoring unheard of in this match so far. There is a moment of alarm early on when Gill produces a genuine Staffordshire cut that sends the ball between his legs and his stumps, but he steadies himself after this and is soon scoring twice as fast as his captain at the other end. Hancock cannot get his timing quite right, is torn between the need for runs and the imperative not to throw his wicket away, wisely settles for a supporting role until his partner has seen them past the half century. Then he goes for aggression himself and, in trying to hook, gets himself caught at square leg. Almost an hour has passed and Staffordshire are just maintaining an adequate rate. One left-handed batsman replaces another, and Gill is joined once again by a man who cannot compete with his verve. It's all very well for Pearsall to drop anchor at the start of his knock, but it soon becomes apparent that he has it stuck in the mud, which is the last thing Staffs need in a situation like this. On the stroke of 6.30, with those 20 overs about to begin, Gill aims to drive another ball and is bowled, having made more than half of Staffordshire's 116 for 2. He has set them well on their way, but can anyone else carry the rest of it off?

Across the road, a couple of women from the terrace are gossiping over their front garden fence, print-aproned and head-scarved, oblivious of the cricket 100 yards away which, having brooded all day, has now begun to flare with life. Nasim, yet another left-hander, comes to the crease with urgency in his tread and straightaway begins to look for quick runs. Pearsall, having decided that the burden shall now be on him alone, and having at last managed to winch his anchor up, repeatedly sends the Indian back. When Staffs have reached 152 he does so once too often and the eager Nasim is easily run out. Within minutes poor Hill meets the same fate without receiving a ball, when Pearsall calls for another one on an overthrow. Then Neal is bowled without scoring and Staffs are suddenly 153 for 5. Something like tension now seizes the ground, although those women across the road are not the only people unaware. Some small boys have taken to cycling round the boundary at the sightscreenless end. They are shouted at vigorously, by umpire, both batsmen, two or three fielders and Northumbrian committee men in a united roar.

Ikin is there now, left-hander again, as his father was. There is too much savvy running in his blood for him to be stranded in midstream as Nasim and Hill were. He looks as decisive and as careful as a partner needs to be with Pearsall in the mood of the past half hour. There are pauses that draw the tension tighter still. A tractor chugs slowly up the farm track, disturbing concentration as the young cyclists did. No one bawls at the driver, but teeth are gritted until he is gone. Pearsall hits 4 past the sightscreen and into the trees beyond. Two fielders and a spectator rummage for the ball but cannot find it and the umpires select a new one while everyone else stands in suspense. Together the batsmen make up the leeway, run for run, while Northumberland's hopes tremble, then teeter, then fall. At the end, with an over or two to spare, it is Ikin who strikes the winning blow, with a late cut and a long-limbed sprint for 3. The Northumbrian committee

men heave a collective sigh and wander over to the pavilion to have one for the road with their hosts. The small
convoy of cars that has assembled since tea growls away
through the gate, and the ground is yielded to the sunset
and a suspicion of evening dew. Staffordshire have put
themselves in good heart for their big match tomorrow at
Stone. But they will want better support than they have
been given today.

### NORTHUMBERLAND—*First Innings*

| | |
|---|---|
| M. YOULL b Ikin | 68 |
| K. PEARSON lbw Gessner | 2 |
| M. E. YOUNGER b Ikin | 47 |
| J. THEWLIS b Nasim | 2 |
| N. C. D. CRAIG b Nasim | 7 |
| R. D. DODDS st Green b Nasim | 7 |
| P. H. TWIZELL lbw Ikin | 1 |
| A. BROWN not out | 16 |
| W. G. ROBSON not out | 26 |
| Extras | 20 |
| | |
| Total (for 7, declared) | 196 |

Fall of wickets: 16, 129, 136, 144, 149, 154, 156.
Did not bat: P. C. Graham, K. Norton.
Bowling: GESSNER 12–4–19–1; LANCASTER 8–2–18–0; NICHOLLS
7–1–21–0; NASIM 23–1–71–3; IKIN 19–5–47–3.

### *Second Innings*

| | |
|---|---|
| M. YOULL run out | 0 |
| K. PEARSON c Green b Lancaster | 5 |
| M. E. YOUNGER lbw Ikin | 63 |
| J. THEWLIS not out | 28 |
| N. C. D. CRAIG b Nicholls | 44 |

R. D. DODDS c Nasim b Nicholls   6
A. BROWN not out   20
   Extras   15

Total (for 5, declared)   181

Fall of wickets: 0, 17, 101, 130, 143.

Bowling: GESSNER 14–3–26–0; LANCASTER 9–4–15–1; NASIM 16–2–51–0; IKIN 28–9–47–1; NICHOLLS 12–4–19–2; GILL 1–0–8–0.

## STAFFORDSHIRE—*First Innings*

D. A. HANCOCK not out   84
P. N. GILL b Norton   37
T. A. PEARSALL not out   64
   Extras   13

Total (for 1, declared)   198

Fall of wicket: 81

Did not bat: Nasim-ul-Ghani, M. R. Hill, S. A. Neal, M. J. Ikin, D. G. Nicholls, M. R. Green, R. Lancaster, B. D. Gessner.

Bowling: GRAHAM 11–1–33–0; TWIZELL 6–0–20–0; NORTON 24–3–65–1; BROWN 17–4–49–0; YOUNGER 2.2–0–18–0.

## *Second Innings*

D. A. HANCOCK c Youll b Brown   21
P. N. GILL b Graham   63
T. A. PEARSALL not out   65
NASIM-UL-GHANI run out   9
M. R. HILL run out   0
S. A. NEAL b Graham   0
M. J. IKIN not out   13
   Extras   10

Total (for 5)   181

Fall of wickets: 59, 116, 152, 153, 153.

Bowling: GRAHAM 11–0–50–2; TWIZELL 7.4–0–38–0; NORTON 11–1–45–0; BROWN 8–0–38–1.

Umpires: N. H. Birch and R. Burrows.

Staffordshire beat Northumberland by 5 wickets.

# Lancashire League

### BACUP v TODMORDEN

THIS, AS NEAR AS MAKES NO MATTER, IS WHERE I DISCOVERED character and splendour in the game; something that elaborated the nervous enjoyment of playing with little distinction at school. I used to cycle up this valley and over these hills to watch cricket on grounds like Lanehead, where the locals would battle with great players from overseas. The epic of Learie Constantine at Nelson was over by then, as was George Headley's time at Haslingden, but Bill Alley was playing for Colne, V. S. Hazare for Rawtenstall; and here, at Bacup, I saw Everton Weekes slaughter the Rishton bowling for 142 not out, and wondered how a human being could be so endowed with such brutal strength. Presently, I also wondered why southerners apparently disapproved of league cricket in the north, with its competitive fire and its paid professional in every team, when they accepted a county championship organised on the same philosophical lines. It was the drama of those Saturday afternoons and the brilliance of those pros that filled the league cricket grounds, as well as rivalry between small Pennine towns that had started with the Industrial Revolution, when they tried to better each other's yarns and cloths. The excitement of those games was why so many Lancashire League followers never went anywhere near Old Trafford, which was thought too far away for convenience and too tame when you got there. They were content with the knowledge that they had seen the likes of Eddie Paynter growing into cricket up here, before going on to do the county and perhaps England a bit of good. Pride in local talent was just as great as admiration of the international men. The League committee presented Eddie with a pair

132

of silver candlesticks when he returned from the bodyline tour, to hallmark that innings in Brisbane, where he got out of a hospital bed and scored 83 with the aid of egg and brandy taken between overs at the crease. Long before Mr Jardine found out, the aldermanic officials of the Enfield club knew that young Paynter had guts.

The most lustrous professional period spanned two decades after the war, which was the age of Lindwall and Simpson, Walcott and Hunte, Dooland and Mankad, Gilchrist and Hall, as well as of Alley, Hazare and Weekes. But the pros are still what they always were in kind, young men with even greater days to come or old timers of infinite wisdom sprung with evergreen. In Bacup v Todmorden today we have just such a pair. Norman O'Neill's son Mark is playing for the home side, only nineteen but in his second season as pro. Todmorden, for their part, have this year enlisted English cricket's most notable encore, the almost eternal Brian Close. After Yorkshire and Somerset, and sometimes England too, he has returned to the high country to play out his career. Of all the League clubs, he will feel easiest working for Tod, which is half in Yorkshire and half in Lancs, a circumstance that accounts for the cricket club's cap badge of crossed roses, one white and one red. It is a stony little place winding along the narrow gap created by a Pennine stream, with a passionate regard for its grammar school, which has produced two Nobel prize-winners, and for its cricket club, which has a membership of 1,000 in a town of 15,000 souls. They don't have divided loyalties in Bacup, or Nobel men, but things over here are much the same in almost every other respect.

In spite of those swaggering memberships, the crowd is on the thin side to see today's contest between David and Goliath and their men. For one thing, it's the last Saturday of Bacup holidays and a lot of folk are still away: for another, the bus service from Todmorden isn't what it used to be, which matters when the backbone of support comes from elderly chaps who never got round to owning cars. A gang of these stalwarts are perched along a bench on the pavilion side when Bacup start to bat, though most eyes are screwed like gimlets on that bald fellow with the Wessex dragon embroidered on his sweater front. For the first few overs, Close does little but bend and rise in the slips, his head creased in thought from the eyebrows almost to the crown. In the Lancashire League this alone can be a provocative act. Out of an ominous silence comes the first observation from the gang: " 'E's gettin' £3,000 for it." Another silence, then another voice along the bench. "I wish I 'ad 'is knowledge." And over the next five minutes, the halting commentary proceeds like this:

"Not doin' any coachin' or anythin', they say."

" 'E's down in London doin' television and comin' up to play wi' this lot Friday neets."

"What's 'e get £3,000 for, then?"

"For bein' called Brian Close."

"They can call me what they like for yon."

" 'E must be a thick-skinned bugger, standin' there doin' nowt for that."

And needs to be, to stand imperturbably within earshot of that bench, when the gate money includes a licence to say what you like as loudly as you will. That old gang, however, are not just picking on Close; their own men are copping it as well. Bacup's opening pair are extremely cautious, uncertain in many of their strokes, and whatever they do or don't gets similar treatment from the bench. After thirty-five minutes and 8 overs they have managed only a dozen runs, which inspires one of these spectators to address his neighbour in disdain. "I'm sure tha could do better wi' a bloody rhubarb stick, Barker." At which Barker grimaces sourly, though he means to say "as like as not". An outsider wouldn't believe these men are enjoying themselves and I'm not sure myself that the phrase adequately covers their participation in the game. They are playing this afternoon as much as any of the cricketers on the field, as inseparable from the distinctive nature of the Lancashire League as its eight-ball overs and its habit of passing round the hat when anyone takes five wickets or scores half a century. They may seem miserable with discontent, but they are playing their parts with the relish of actors who know their lines and never miss a cue. One of them hands round a bag of humbugs, which comes back to him with not many left. "Christ," he says, peering at the remainder, "I'll bring dolly mixtures next time." Lanehead is dotted with groups like this, platforms of denunciation tilted between heaven and earth. The ground has a slope that makes Lord's seem as flat as a pancake, which follows from the contours 1,000 feet up. At Todmorden they play beside the riverbed. At Bacup, the Victorians rolled out their pitch where sheep grazed between drystone walls. Bracing is the word for it, even when the cricket is slow.

The first wicket falls at 19 and this brings in O'Neill, to shouts of "Come on Mark, let's 'ave some today." He hasn't been doing too well with the bat so far, an average of 25.33 in 17 innings, which is lower than that of any other professional in the League; but Close's average is only 31.4 and the young Australian has been doing better than him with the ball. O'Neill is a stocky, curly-headed man, only facially resembling Sydney's illustrious Draw-card Norm. Father was usually a nervous starter but, in this company at least, son is not. In his first over he hits 3 through the covers, then 4 past point, and soon the numbers are revolving on the scoreboard, a two-storey brick edifice that looks like a branch-line signal box. The 50 comes up in just over an hour with both batsmen now going for runs; as they need to, with only 34 overs to the innings, which must be completed in two-and-a-half-hours of play. If the weather intrudes, though, the match will be settled on the number of runs scored per over, which is the Lancashire League's way of leaning over backwards to secure a result. And today, the weather might have its say. The sunshine that started the game has disappeared in top haze and the Union Jack outside the pavilion hangs dankly from its flagstaff, smelling of rain.

At 55 for 1, Brian Close bowls his first ball. So far he has been a focal point of comment, a stirring of memory, but little else. He has not exerted himself in the slips, has seemed almost to be watching the cricket from the wings.

Now and then he has made small gestures to other fieldsmen, who have obediently altered position a few yards, this way or that. He has been very discreet in doing this. Close, after all, is not the captain of the side and even his overwhelmingly greater experience must be sold to his employers with tact. Both he and Jim Clayton there understand this subtle relationship between a captain and his pro; neither appears as bossman, each lets the other take a lead. But when Close comes on to bowl, his stature in the team becomes overt. He marshals the field as a commander would troops, while Clayton stands adjutant, watching the expert at work. Backsides shift expectantly on benches all round the ground, as they might if this were theatre with Olivier making his first entrance in the lead.

The first over is a disaster. Nicholson hits the third ball for 4 and, smack on cue, one of Barker's mates shouts "Send 'im some more o' them!" The fifth ball is clouted high towards an outfielder, who drops it and sees it roll down the slope across the ropes. The eight balls cost 10 runs, and Close trudges back to his place in the slips with head histrionically bent and a gritty expression on his face. He looked as if he'd already had enough when that catch was dropped. His second over has the batsmen puzzled, O'Neill playing very carefully at the spin, but Bacup are 70 for 1 when Close comes up for a third bout with his rival pro. Round the wicket he wheels, slaps the Australian on the pad and turns-about like a dervish with a roaring "How's that!" ("Look in t' *Pink 'un* toneet!" is the advice from Barker's bench.) Not out. Another two balls, another slap on the pads, another appeal, and this time the umpire's finger goes up. O'Neill seems stunned, points to where the ball pitched, shouts something that is lost in the discord from spectators at either end. He turns and slowly walks away, impatiently wrenching off his gloves, but keeps looking back to where Brian Close is grinning like the cat who stole the cream.

The Bacup innings declines abruptly after that, so that we don't get much sight of young Ashworth, who has been playing a bit for the Lancashire Second XI. Not until the home side have been reduced to 92 for 7 is there a sign of anyone damming the flow of Todmorden's attack. Close has bowled another man in this time, has tempted a third so far from his crease that he is easily stumped. But now he is assaulted himself, when Cahill hits out at everything and connects with most, in an effort to cram as many more runs in the book before the ration of overs is spent. Close is fielding at mid-off when the first 6 soars into the pavilion seats; but half a dozen balls later the old warrior himself is knocked clean out of the ground. Two quick steps and Cahill has driven the ball straight back over Close's head, past the scoreboard, over the white-washed stone wall, full toss into a front garden across the side street. "Another sixpenn'orth, is it?" Barker exclaims as the ball, still rising, flies over the Lanehead wall. This is what the old gang have hoped to see. Not just Bacup putting up a show to leave a respectable score for the visitors to face, but one of their own lads knocking the high and mighty about. Close should know his northern crowds better than to stand there with a look of disgust. It only adds to the relish of knowing he's been hit where it hurts. He can't be too happy with a bowling average of 19.92, when ten of the thirteen other league professionals are higher up the table than him.

What Tod have to face in the end is 124 for 7, which isn't much of a score on small grounds like this, especially when they have a slope that draws balls to one boundary like a magnet. The hard club drinkers are down at that end of the ground, in a reconstituted prefab left over from some post-war housing drive. It fills noisily during the interval between the innings. So does the refreshment room at the top of the slope, where temperance reigns, and plenty to eat. The Lancashire League has always taken the view that good digestion aids appreciation of the game, and there are many pages in its handbook telling patrons to "Enjoy your cricket with Holland's pies and puddings", or attend to their victuals in other ways. The windows are steamed up in there by the time play starts again, with all the brewing of tea and gossip that's been going on. Outside, the temperature has dropped sharply, and heavy cloud has begun to roll up Rossendale. After only two overs of the Todmorden innings, rain comes swashing across the hill on the other side of the valley, obscuring the pylons that stride over its bracken and its drystone enclosures. The downpour doesn't last long at Lanehead, but it drives the players from the field, spectators back to refreshments, and keeps us all waiting for nearly an hour after it has stopped. The umpires, meanwhile, come out to inspect the turf and, when they decide play can't start at once, they are barracked by Barker and Co, who haven't paid 55p to gawp at that pigeon loft on the hillside across. At half-past five the players are allowed out again, get another two overs in, then disappear in a second squall. This does less damage than the first and by six o'clock the game is at last on its way. But now its whole rhythm has been changed. Only ninety minutes are left for play and Tod must keep their eyes on run-rate, not on Bacup's final score.

The openers set to with a will, on a field dappled with sawdust, against bowlers who towel practically every ball they send. Inside ten minutes the first wicket goes and, one run later, Bacup's keeper takes a blinding catch low down and far away to his left, to make Todmorden 19 for 2. Enter Close, to the bowling of O'Neill. He comes out of the pavilion chewing gum, that great dome of a head layered with the furrows of nearly thirty years in the game. Is it crossing his mind, perhaps, that the end of the road cannot be far away, now that he is tilting with a man who couldn't have been walking when his father played Test match cricket against Close? Can he make this latest encore last, spinning out the guile and the strength, the bloody-mindedness and the plain old-fashioned courage for a few more years? Or is it almost goodbye Mr Chips, with the eye not what it was, the body no longer so responsive to instinct's call, the generations crowding in? Brian Close has been so durable, so liable to astonish us with the resources for yet another heroic role, that we have been apt to forget that he, too, is ultimately bound by mortal flesh and blood. He looks tired when he comes out to bat this evening. From a few chimney pots below the ground, smoke begins to curl into the rain-rinsed sky, as if to signal a twilight time.

He swings cross-batted at the first delivery he gets from O'Neill and, though it isn't the same stroke he kept making, fatally at last, to Benaud in 1961, it has something of the same impulse to sweep away a torment or be damned. He misses that ball, but firmly plays back the last two deliveries down the pitch. He is still there when O'Neill's next over starts, fastish stuff slung down with all the leaping spirit of nineteen years. He straight drives the first ball and, although it only earns a single, there is in that stroke all the old belligerence, all the sudden release of strength whiplashed out of Close's brain. He was never one for patting the ground nervously with his bat while he waited for the ball to come. He still doesn't do it, but he runs very carefully when he must these days, middle-aged man anxious not to fall. Before that over is done, he straight drives again and this time doesn't need to run as the ball whizzes past the sightscreen and bangs against the wall. "Good shot, Brian," someone shouts; which is the first friendly remark he will have heard from Bacup all day.

The score mounts, for Stansfield is getting runs, too. But it is the duel between the two professionals which, more often than not, decides the outcome in league cricket. Close seems to be getting the better of this one when he takes his score to 13 with another boundary off O'Neill, lifting the ball over leg slip's head with a swivel of the wrists. Then he's hit on the pads and O'Neill, bursting to redress a grievance, turns and bellows "How is *that!*" at the umpire responsible for his own disputed end. Not out; and Close strikes the next ball down the slope for 3, just to rub it in. The entire Bacup team, indeed, have been appealing at almost every ball Close has received and failed to punch cleanly away, paying him back for what they reckon was just an old lag's trick that happened to come off. But it is Close's forty-six years that finish his innings today, not anything Bacup's cricketers have done. He is on 18 when Stansfield chips a ball from Fell through slips. Some lingering sprite inside Brian Close makes him call for a single and he sets off on long legs towards the striker's end. Stansfield dashes past him before he is half-way there, already a slip has turned and has the ball, and those long legs are too stiff to carry Close to safety in time. He thunders past the broken wicket and carries on for several yards, head flung back in anguish at the loss of what was once so easily gained. Then he turns and comes in, grim-faced as he could be even in his salad days, but now with his chest heaving out of breath.

Tod are still in with a chance, at 50 for 3, and just about up with the necessary rate. And all Bacup tenses at the prospect of that palpitating finish to a cricket match that has been the making of the Lancashire League. It becomes hit and run, swing and slash, and fieldsmen racing desperately to every part of the ground, or poised menacing as man-traps near the bat. First-class cricket never knew the like until a few years ago, but this is much the same game the counties now play every weekend in the John Player League. And for all its great exuberance and its throwing of caution to the winds, it is not so very far behind the technical accomplishments of those county men. It is a cut or two above the robust finishes you are likely to see on the average village green. The crowd, using its lungs to exhort or decry everything that's done, haven't come merely to see Close and O'Neill put on a turn. They expect value for money from the amateurs as well; and generally speaking, give or take a fumbled ball and an optimistic stroke, they get what they've come for tonight.

Wickets fall regularly, as they must in such an excited pass, but there is some splendid hitting in reply. Hartley, Todmorden's Number Six, gets going like a good 'un and, for the second time in the match, the ball is put mightily out of the ground with such a tremendous blow that from 150 yards away it looks as if it cleared not only the wall but the house across the side street as well. A long pause before it is retrieved, and heads around the ground are still being shaken in acknowledgment of that one when it comes back. Hartley's partner is hit on the pads and, when the umpire who gave O'Neill out puts his finger up for the first time since, he gets a loud ironic cheer. The next man is also rapped, and half the Bacup team go "Ooh!" as though in pain themselves. Some people might not regard this as cricket, and would not exonerate those players just because Tod have reached 84 for 6, with five league table points at stake, but here it is thought excusable and known as being keen. Bacup's captain is the keenest of them all, chivvying his men to plug the gaps and hold the fort, aware of the time factor, hungry for a win. O'Neill collects the ball from the pavilion rails and trots back to his place at mid-wicket before tossing it to the bowler. His captain, not much older than him, claps his hands sharply and calls "Come on Mark. Hurry up!" There are two or three hundred others around Lanehead beginning to get on edge, now that Tod are within striking distance of victory. Another 20 runs or so at this rate and the match will be theirs.

Nowhere is the climax followed more intently than up that wooden ladder and inside the top floor of the signal box. The small boy who puts numbers on the scoreboard, a Bacup player's son, kneels by his peephole and watches solemnly as the cricketers settle his honour for the week. The detritus of a season is ranged along a shelf by his side, thirty empties which once contained Ben Shaw's Cola, Orange Squash and Raspberry Flavour, now gathering dust. He keeps an ear cocked for instructions from the scorers, sitting at their table in a corner of the box, behind a large window tucked under the eaves. Tod's man is one of the League's great statistical buffs, for ever totting things up and entering arcane achievements in different coloured books. When rain stopped play he was working out averages, getting his records squared off. Now, between pencilling marks on the official scorebook, he is dabbing at a pocket calculator, trying to reckon Tod's rate of advance compared with Bacup's. At 90 for 8 after 23 overs, with fifteen minutes left, he has his work cut out. This is going to be a very close run thing. A reporter comes up the ladder and telephones the news to the Todmorden ground at Centre Vale, where the two Second XIs are playing today. He's still on the line when young Ash-

141

worth takes a splendid running catch near the boundary to make Tod's First XI 97 for 9. "Tell 'em," says Todmorden's scorer, "they need 8 runs off t' last three overs." He looks up at the field, where not many spectators are sitting on benches now. Lanehead is fringed with people standing urgently, shouting and calling advice. It's like the finish of a hound trail up in the Lakes.

Bacup have placed their hopes on the medium pace of Fell and on Cahill, a grey-headed man who comes to the crease on tiptoe with leg-spin, which has not yet vanished from the Lancashire League. It has bought the wicket that Ashworth caught out and it even has the obstinate Hartley groping most of the time. But he manages another boundary off Cahill's last ball, leaving a couple of overs still to be bowled and only 4 runs to win the match. Todmorden's Number Eleven has faced nothing yet, Hartley having made sure of that by crossing and staying put when the ninth wicket fell, with the long nose of experience in tight spots like this. He has a word with his partner before Fell comes to bowl, while voices round the boundary tell them to "Geddonwithit!" And for six balls, with every Bacup fieldsman crouching fiercely within yards of his bat, Whitaker does his part. He misses four deliveries, blocks down two more, which is almost all he needs to do with Hartley ready to take Cahill's final over from the other end. Perhaps it is merely tension that makes him swing at Fell's penultimate ball, or maybe he has a sudden inspiration that he, not Hartley, can win this match for Tod. Swing he does, sending the ball through that tight infield, himself galloping towards the other end, heedless of Hartley's warning to get back. For O'Neill has pivoted at short extra-cover, cut off the ball and picked it up in two strides, turned and started to throw before Whitaker can even bring himself to a standstill face to Hartley's frantic face. The Australian's throw goes straight into the keeper's gloves as he rushes to the stumps, the bails are off and every Bacup fielder springs upwards in delight. And a great roar of triumph goes round the boundaries and volleys off Lanehead's stone walls. It dies down, while people slap Bacup backs as the players come in. In the quietness that follows, the sound of a cock crowing carries from across the valley, where a farm track gleams wetly on the moorland flank.

## BACUP

| | |
|---|---:|
| P. NICHOLSON lbw Whitaker | 36 |
| J. C. DAVIES b Townsend | 8 |
| O'NEILL lbw Close | 25 |
| R. LAW c Smith b Whitaker | 0 |
| P. LORD st Stansfield b Close | 3 |
| S. ASHWORTH b Close | 10 |
| G. CAHILL run out | 30 |
| P. FELL not out | 4 |
| Extras | 8 |
| Total (for 7, 34 overs) | 124 |

Fall of wickets: 19, 70, 76, 79, 81, 92.
Did not bat: F. Mitchell, G. Simcock, P. Clarke.
Bowling: TOWNSEND 8–2–21–1; HARTLEY 5–1–13–0; WILKINS 2–0–16–0; WHITAKER 9–0–34–2; CLOSE 10–3–32–3.

## TODMORDEN

| | |
|---|---:|
| I. SMITH c Nicholson b Fell | 12 |
| A. FIDDLING c Mitchell b O'Neill | 6 |
| G. STANSFIELD c Lord b Clarke | 21 |
| CLOSE run out | 18 |
| J. E. CLAYTON b Fell | 3 |
| M. HARTLEY not out | 27 |
| J. BRIERLEY lbw Fell | 4 |
| T. GREENWOOD lbw Fell | 0 |
| J. TOWNSEND b Fell | 0 |
| J. WILKINS c Ashworth b Cahill | 6 |
| R. WHITAKER run out | 0 |
| Extras | 4 |
| Total | 101 |

Fall of wickets: 18, 19, 50, 59, 67, 84, 90, 90, 97.

Bowling: O'NEILL 8–2–38–1; FELL 13.7–2–25–5; CLARKE 3–0–18–1; CAHILL 3–0–16–1.

Umpires: Turner and Gregory.

Bacup beat Todmorden by 23 runs.

# Canterbury Week

### KENT v WARWICKSHIRE

IF I HAD TO SHOW A FOREIGNER HIS FIRST CRICKET MATCH, I
should ideally like it to be here, during Canterbury Week.
Such introductions have generally taken place in the
setting of Lord's and the foreigners, though still per-
plexed by the game itself, have usually gone away
impressed by the accommodation and the discovery that
this is the headquarters of an international sport. At
Canterbury they would not find matters so grand, but
there are some things more visible here than at Lord's that
I would much rather convey. Most of all, perhaps, the fact
that first-class cricket has not put too much distance
between itself and the more modest levels of the game.
Apart from its superior skills, it differs remarkably little
in atmosphere from the village green and the league or
non-league cricket club. It has kept in touch with its
origins and with the generality of people from whom all
cricket springs in a way that has become increasingly rare
among the big spectator sports; sports, that is, capable of
attracting tens of thousands to a single event. A First
Division football club and its team are insulated from their
environment and their supporters both physically and
philosophically, and they have all left their beginnings a
long way behind. The same goes for an American baseball
club in the major leagues. But an English county cricket
club is still all of a piece with its past, still in touch with a
present that includes all the people and elements on which it
is built. In this sense, for all the snobberies that linger yet,
cricket may be the most nearly democratic of games. You can
see all this quite clearly during Canterbury Week.

Kent come to this match as joint champions of England,
a title they will hold alone by the season's end if they can

stave off the challenge of Essex, who must by now be the only county capable of overtaking them at the top. Before play starts, their cricketers, together with Warwickshire's men, practise in front of the pavilion, which is but a larger and more elegant version of the pavilion I saw up in Bacup last week. Its main structural difference is the seating for a few dozen people one storey high, sandwiched between the roof's dormer clock and the verandah which shelters as many more. I don't suppose a brick has been changed, or one of those cast-iron posts, or that fretwork decorating the roof, since the St Lawrence Ground was opened in 1847. True, there is a modern annexe alongside, containing offices and dressing rooms, and this pair of buildings are themselves flanked by two stands, one looking as old as the pavilion, the other dedicated to Frank Woolley in concrete with a cantilevered thrust. The whole group has the same organic charm that English High Streets invariably had before developers tore whole blocks down to make way for something more profitable and uniformly dull. Those cricketers are batting and bowling to each other on the grass just in front. So are scores of boys and some of their Dads. Nets have not been erected to separate the great men from those who have come to imitate and admire. It is just happening, rhythmically and untidily, with everyone carefully not treading on anybody else's toes. Three of those cricketers are among the highest-paid professionals in the world, and at least two of them have played to a crowd of getting on for 100,000 before now. No one dreams of interrupting this start to their day's work. This is as far from the preamble to a football match at Highbury or White Hart Lane as you could possibly get.

Ealham has won the toss and decided to bat on a pitch that will be slow after recent rain. Bob Woolmer is missing with a sore arm, which balances Warwick's loss of Willis, who is en route for Trent Bridge and tomorrow's Test. So we see Johnson and Rowe coming out first, making their way on to the field through part of the crowd, as cricketers always do, with never the slightest chance that they will be impeded by enthusiasm or partisan spirit gone daft (though getting back can sometimes be another matter at close of play in these demonstrative days). There are spots of rain in the air as Brown comes up to bowl the first ball, but we ignore them at once when Johnson hits it for 4 past third man; have forgotten their existence when he takes another 3 before the over's end. This is the way festival cricket should begin and Canterbury Week, having first happened in 1842 on the Beverley ground, is the oldest cricket festival of them all. Not that the two games played each year are as festive as those between invitation sides up at Scarborough every September. Championship points are always at stake at Canterbury in August, which puts a brake on giving the customers fireworks from beginning to end. Johnson, evidently startled by the velocity of his takeoff, suddenly remembers Kent's priorities when that first over is done, and doesn't score another run for nearly an hour. In that time Rowe, delicately picking balls off his toes with mostly on-side strokes, brings his own score up to 17. By then Warwickshire have lost the services of Brown, who skids on a damp patch during his follow-through, falls full length and leaves the field with something of a limp.

The start is placid after Johnson's brief headlong rush. The crowd quietly absorbs not only the play but the particular impregnations of the festival Week. This is at all times one of the most attractive county grounds, with a suggestion of parkland space formed by trees and grassy banks, as remote as could be from a stadium for a sport. When the Week comes round it is given a jubilee air, or something in common with an agricultural show, with the pegging down of tents and marquees and the fluttering of their flags. There are fifteen of them this year, stretched between mid-wicket and long-on where the ground borders the Old Dover Road. The Mayor of Canterbury has set himself up in one, the President of Kent (the cricket club, that is) in another. The Association of the Men of Kent and Kentish Men reconciles its differences under one canvas roof. Another is shared by the Queen's Own Buffs and the Old Stagers, whose amateur theatricals have traditionally taken to the boards when the cricketers have left the field, though advertisement points to other frivolities after close of play; the loudspeaker system has been informing us that there will be a wine and cheese party tonight, and on the pavilion door a notice threatens dancing with music by Brass Roots. Each of these marquees has a small enclosure in front, from which the cricket is watched, with swathes of gladioli or roses or carnations marking territorial limits. Each has its flagstaff with distinctive bunting at the top. Some of these look like old school ties, all stripes diagonally placed. Others resemble those tricoloured national flags whose countries you can never recall. Between them, they represent a considerable section of life in the county of Kent.

At 12.20 Whitehouse drops Rowe off Rouse in the slips, the batsman then being on 20, with Johnson having by now added a small clutch to his initial score. It is he who, 2 runs later, nudges Perryman into the covers and calls his partner for a quick one; but Rowe is not quick enough off the mark and is run out with plenty to spare. This, at 41 for 1, seems to prick Johnson into new life and in the next over he takes 8 runs off Rouse. It also brings in Tavaré, who appears to be wearing a protective device I've never seen before, a gum shield no less. Perhaps we shall be excited now, for Tavaré is having a good season, well up the batting averages and spoken of as a possibility for the winter's Australian tour. The ground is filling agreeably, though the sky is dull, and Canterbury is whetted for the elegance of the slim young man. In the boxes of the stand dedicated to Leslie Ames, well-dressed gents are already convivial with drink, the ledges over-hanging the field impressively loaded with pints and with shorts. Inside the marquee enclosures, almost every deck-chair is occupied by people with the right connections over there. The grassy banks are virtually obscured by cars that now circle the ground, from which chairs and even tables will presently be withdrawn, so that lunch can be taken *al fresco* but with home comfort as well. On the benches ranged below the banks, sandwiches and Mars bars are more likely to be the order of the day, for this is where the hoi polloi of Canterbury pass the Week.

Aha, the foreigner will say (and many of the English, too), so this crowd is divided into the privileged and the rest? And you dare to claim that this is a democratic sport? I do indeed, because the privilege only goes as far as you can see. A number of notices are displayed on the St Lawrence Ground, inviting spectators to become members of the county club. There are no qualifications for this beyond an ability to tip up an £8 subscription, which will not only entitle you to watch all home matches free of charge, in any of the seating provided by the club, but will also give you a vote at an annual meeting to pick the committee that regulates all the affairs of county cricket in Kent. Those committee men don't take a penny out of the game for doing this; and there is not one soul on this ground who can't, if he wishes, have a say in deciding who they shall be. Try putting that proposition to the next shareholders' meeting of your professional football club; but first try to buy your qualifying share. Entire cricket committees have been swept away before now because there has been a popular vote that they must go. It happened up at Old Trafford in 1964.

There are Kent members on this bench alongside me and I guess that they are here rather than in one of the privileged stands because this is where they have chosen to be. Some of us prefer this proximity to the play, where nothing but a flimsy billboard and our own restraint prevents us from joining the players on the field. We can have a word with Kallicharran at his boundary post after each ball is bowled, and he will doubtless chat back so long as the conversation isn't too long; outfielders usually do, however exalted they are. He tenses in forward reflex as the batsman shapes a powerful stroke, in that moment of flourish when there is no telling where the ball will be sent; but this one is not for the West Indian to stop. Tavaré has driven so beautifully straight that the ball, on its way to the boundary, throws up a puff of sawdust from the pile by the bowler's mark. Then Johnson is bowled with his head in the air and, at 66 for 2, Asif Iqbal comes out swinging his bat. He is a plunderer, Asif, with a decep-

149

tively amiable face. Watch him in conversation with the umpire, beaming smiles and radiating fellowship on all; but if he gets after these bowlers he'll make them smart. And in the fifteen minutes before lunch he shows them what to expect, with a cracking drive off Perryman and a dashing between the stumps for 4.

It is then that filthy black cloud begins to ooze across the sky in the distance, just above the tower of Becket's cathedral, behind the pavilion and nearby stands. While lunch is on, and while young spectators play their own cricket on the field, this darkness draws nearer. It has become so gloomy by the time the players reappear that the umpires give the batsmen the option of retiring again; but they considerately decide to have a go. Within minutes the bad light probably costs Asif his wicket, when he plays too soon at Rouse and plonks the ball gently into cover's hands. As he walks away, the first roll of thunder rumbles up the road. Before Ealham reaches the crease, the rain starts and he turns back, pursued by all Warwickshire, Tavaré and the umpires. They barely get inside before a deluge breaks, a downpour of such force that mud is splashed a foot or more into the air.

It doesn't last long, but it doesn't need to in order to wreck the middle of Canterbury Week. It is quite some time before the umpires bother to inspect the streaming field and announce that they'll take another look in a couple of hours. People emerge from dripping canvas and steamed-up cars, and adapt themselves to the waiting game. Books are opened, conversations are struck up, exercise is taken and the refreshment tent is packed to its seams. I wander round the ground and pause by the memorial to Colin Blythe – Cockney, violinist and spin bowler – who volunteered in time to be at Ypres and never came back. Once again I find myself with a cricketing ghost, thoughtful at the past, enormously warmed by the present, more anxious than I would wish to be for what the future may bring. Kent and Warwickshire, more than most counties, remind me why this should be so because both have been writhing lately over the issues raised by the Packer affair. Kent have just decided to re-engage Woolmer, Asif, Underwood and Knott for another year in spite of their affiliations with the Australian tycoon. But Warwickshire have chosen to chuck Amiss out, though many members are against it and heaven knows how the democracy will settle things there in the end. There are few straightforward answers to the conundrum Packer has posed.

In one respect, and in only one I think, he has done a service to the game by forcing us all to face the fact that cricketers have been abysmally ill-paid. It is scandalous that so good and faithful a player as Bob Stephenson of Hants is obliged to repair cricket gloves in order to make both ends meet. The question of where decent pay packets are to come from has a variety of answers, but we who watch cricket should certainly be supplying one of them, for we have had this part of our life on the cheap for too long, none of us more than county members. The subscription to the Hambledon club in 1791 was three guineas a year, which was the same amount required for membership of Hampshire County Cricket Club in 1965, and after thirteen years of inflation it is still no more than £10. This is ridiculous, given the value of money today, and what a member gets in return, and the fact that most members are by definition people of means enough to let them watch cricket in the middle of a week. I have every sympathy with players who have baulked at this lop-sided state of affairs and gone for more money than English cricket could or would provide. At the same time I wish they had tried to redress the imbalance in other ways. I do not believe that in the long run Mr Packer will do much good for anyone who cherishes the game.

It is to him a means of making money and exerting power above all else. These are perfectly respectable ambitions and there are respected names in the government of English cricket who enjoy the second in their own way. But they are not ambitions which, in tandem, can exist near cricket's heart and be content with its peculiar combination of aggression and gentleness, with its unfashionable morality, with its tenderness for its past, with its reluctance to leave behind the things which it

151

esteems. They are not consonant with the subtle tones of this game. One of Mr Packer's defects is that he does not appear to have an original thought in his head, unless it was the one which would have fielders standing within concentric circles "to speed up the game". Most of the ideas he would inflict on cricket have been borrowed from the United States and are traceable to professional baseball, from its comically mis-named World Series to its habit of playing night games under floodlight with the use of white balls. Baseball is a very fine game, not to be spoken of patronisingly as ignorant Englishmen too often do, but it has been badly polluted by commerce. So much money is at stake that almost anything goes in an effort to attract massive crowds, from the merely garish to the downright unpleasant. Cartooned handclaps flash on to electronic scoreboards to applaud home runs. Wurlitzer organs play while the game is taking place on the field. Brawls are not uncommon in full view of the crowd, between players whose own scramble for dollars transcends any notion of sport. At almost every other game you watch, a team manager will rush out of the dug-out and hector an umpire, sometimes physically, in front of the howling mob. I have seen fans empty popcorn over a visiting player when he has been trying to catch a high ball under the bleachers wall. Players are traded between teams with even more abandon than in the English Football League, having no say in whether they stay or go: they do what the club owner wishes or they lose their livelihood.

I do not want to see any of this poison in cricket, but I fear that we might if the game were to be rearranged on Mr Packer's lines. I prefer it the way it is in Canterbury Week, even when rain has stopped play for the day (as it turns out) with Kent on 77 for 3, and I can't return to see the rest of the match. I like the way those two Warwickshire cricketers can amble round this civilised ground, killing time while the umpires make up their minds, nodding matily to people who nod back and sometimes say a word but are perhaps too shy to start up a conversation, not wishing to intrude. I rejoice in the continuity of a gathering in the President's tent this afternoon, when a handful of Kent's old-timers sauntered over and had a drink. Doug Wright was there, and Jack Martin, and a trio of the county's extraordinary sequence of fine keepers; "Hopper" Levett, great Ames himself, and Godfrey Evans who, as the years go on, looks more and more like mine host, mutton-chops and all, of a tavern on the stage-coach run down the Dover Road.

Canterbury has a living symbol of the values that I would protect in this game. Down at third man, in front of the tents, its famous lime tree grows a good ten yards inside the normal boundary. Judged by the Mitchell test (an inch of girth for each year, five feet above the ground) it must be something like 150 years old. In other words, when the St Lawrence Ground was first used for cricket and its boundaries were marked, that tree stood inconveniently as a sapling in the area of play. The temptation to remove it must have been great, especially as there were other saplings nearby. But those old men of Kent let it be because it was a fine thing, and eventually devised ground rules to accommodate its occasional obstruction of the ball. Their successors have never dreamed of removing it, have been happy to see it reach its full nobility and height. Mr Packer, I suspect, would have chopped it down long ago, so that a few more spectators could thereby be given a view of play, a few more pounds be taken at the Canterbury gate. He would have argued that there were plenty more lime trees where that came from. But there aren't.

KENT—*First Innings*

| | |
|---|---|
| G. W. JOHNSON b Clifford | 30 |
| C. J. C. ROWE run out | 21 |
| C. J. TAVARÉ c Lloyd b Clifford | 13 |
| ASIF IQBAL c Oliver b Rouse | 5 |
| A. G. E. EALHAM c Humpage b Brown | 24 |
| J. N. SHEPHERD b Clifford | 21 |
| C. S. COWDREY c Humpage b Brown | 15 |

| | |
|---|---:|
| R. W. HILLS c Lloyd b Clifford | 10 |
| P. R. DOWNTON lbw Brown | 11 |
| D. L. UNDERWOOD c and b Brown | 25 |
| K. B. S. JARVIS not out | 5 |
| Extras (b 1, nb 6, w 1, nb 7) | 15 |

Total                                          195

Fall of wickets: 41, 66, 77, 81, 114, 132, 153, 153, 176.
Bowling: BROWN 13.2–3–49–4; ROUSE 15–6–44–1; PERRYMAN 16–3–25–0; CLIFFORD 23–5–77–4.


## Second Innings

| | |
|---|---:|
| G. W. JOHNSON run out | 44 |
| C. J. C. ROWE c Kallicharran b Perryman | 42 |
| C. J. TAVARÉ c Lloyd b Oliver | 0 |
| ASIF IQBAL not out | 28 |
| A. G. E. EALHAM not out. | 0 |
| Extras (b 4, lb 1, w 1, nb 1) | 8 |

Total (for 3, declared)                        122

Fall of wickets: 73, 73, 113.
Bowling: ROUSE 6–2–19–0; PERRYMAN 5–3–9–1; CLIFFORD 14–9–52–0; OLIVER 14–5–34–1.


## WARWICKSHIRE—*First Innings*

| | |
|---|---:|
| D. L. AMISS lbw Underwood | 13 |
| K. D. SMITH lbw Underwood | 15 |
| A. KALLICHARRAN c Ealham b Underwood | 16 |
| S. J. ROUSE st Downton b Johnson | 2 |
| J. WHITEHOUSE c Cowdrey b Underwood | 47 |
| T. A. LLOYD b Johnson | 0 |
| G. W. HUMPAGE c Downton b Underwood | 8 |

| | |
|---|---|
| P. R. OLIVER c Johnson b Underwood | 18 |
| D. J. BROWN b Underwood | 2 |
| C. C. CLIFFORD lbw Johnson | 0 |
| S. J. PERRYMAN not out | 0 |
| Extras (b 4, lb 3, nb 2) | 9 |
| Total | 130 |

Fall of wickets: 23, 47, 50, 52, 52, 64, 127, 129, 130.

Bowling: JARVIS 4–0–33–0; SHEPHERD 2–1–9–0; JOHNSON 18–2–41–3; UNDERWOOD 19.1–9–38–7.

## Second Innings

| | |
|---|---|
| D. L. AMISS c Asif b Underwood | 5 |
| K. D. SMITH c Cowdrey b Johnson | 15 |
| A. KALLICHARRAN b Underwood | 29 |
| J. WHITEHOUSE not out | 9 |
| T. A. LLOYD c Tavaré b Johnson | 1 |
| S. J. ROUSE not out | 0 |
| Extras (b 3, nb 2) | 5 |
| Total (for 4) | 64 |

Fall of wickets: 23, 23, 60, 63.

Bowling: JARVIS 1–0–4–0; SHEPHERD 1–0–4–0; JOHNSON 25–13–25–2; UNDERWOOD 22–14–25–2; ROWE 3–2–1–0.

Umpires: B. J. Meyer and K. E. Palmer.

Kent (5 points) drew with Warwickshire (4 points).

# Cup Final

### SOMERSET v SUSSEX

THE GILLETTE CUP FINAL COMMANDS MORE NATIONAL attention now, in its sixteenth year, than any other cricket match outside a Test. It has all the potential excitement of the one-day game and of the climax to a knock-out competition, and that climax comes where it logically should, in a metropolitan flourish just before the season's end. It packs Lord's to capacity every year and tickets are almost as hard to come by as those for the footballers' Cup Final at Wembley in May; you apply for them months in advance or you make do with a television set on the day. It brings supporting casts in thousands from the two counties playing for the cup, ready and willing to make this a memorable event in their own way. Wurzel Gummidge figures in smocks, Taunton shepherds with crooks, are to be seen gallivanting by the Tavern in dozens this morning, and banners begin to appear all over the ground as we pour into the sunlit arena and catch sight of players heading for the pavilion after practice at the Nursery nets. A great roar from Somerset folk as Joel Garner strides across in seven-league boots, and a great gasp from many who've never clapped eyes on him until now. He's six foot eight inches high, a giant in every respect, and cricket can't often have seen his like before.

But the strength of that roar is the more significant thing today. There must be ten West Country men at Lord's for every supporter from Sussex, judging by the row; which is no more than a reflection of where the balance is thought to lie between these teams. The bookies are backing Somerset to win at 7 to 4, but by popular account they are much hotter favourites than that. They beat Warwickshire, Glamorgan and Kent in some style on the way to Lord's and their semi-final was one of the most thrilling matches ever played, a tied game with Essex which they won on fewer wickets lost. Sussex had a soft start against minor counties in the first two rounds (beating Staffordshire by only 2 runs in the second), followed by a narrow victory over Yorkshire in a ten-overs slog before trouncing Lancashire in the semi-final at Hove. Somerset are having the best season in their history. Their challenge for the championship fell away a week or two ago, but by tomorrow night they could be Gillette Cupholders and winners of the John Player League.* For Sussex it has been a wretched year until this last month, and most of the misery has followed in Mr Packer's wake, with dissension tearing at the innards of the club. As the county go into their Cup Final at Lord's, those old Sussex heroes, Greig and Snow, are playing exhibition cricket at a baseball stadium in New York.

It will be the chance of early moisture in the pitch that has persuaded Arnold Long to put Somerset in to bat, but it seems a brave thing to be doing against such a powerful scoring side, even if it is five years since the cup went to the team batting first. And a blundering misjudgment, perhaps, when Brian Rose takes 14 runs off Imran's opening over. The smocked figures fringeing the outfield are up and dancing with West Indian gusto at each of their captain's three boundary strokes, and the hullabaloo has scarcely subsided by the time Denning has played out a maiden from Arnold at the Nursery end. But nerves are twitching in Somerset's ranks this morning and, after almost being run out, Denning is bowled without getting a run. Which is to say that, inside half an hour, Viv Richards comes out to the acclaim kept for men known to be capable of settling cricket matches by themselves. "Here's the one who's going to win it for us," says a rosy lady on my left. "My God, he's got to," says an anxious voice nearby, its owner pouring himself a drink to stiffen that nerve. "'E's only 'uman, same as everybody else,"

*Hampshire, in fact, won the Sunday League on a higher run rate throughout the season. Somerset lost their last match, and with it the trophy, to Essex by 2 runs.

says an old chap in a straw hat, who can remember the days of Jack White and all the dashed hopes Somerset have known before and since. Richards has walked to the crease crisply, buttoned up at the cuffs and almost to the chin, with none of the rangy slouch of Clive Lloyd, who otherwise most resembles him in a cricketing sense. Richards is compact, a man built of coiled muscle that lets fly with lightning force if need be, though a glittering eye generally allows time for more leisurely action than that. Off Imran's third ball he drives 4 runs to the long-on ropes so lazily that I almost expect him to finish the stroke with hand to mouth, stifling a yawn. The last ball from Imran he hooks at wickedly, perfectly executing the stroke, except that it doesn't connect. That one over shows all the temper, all the spectacular reflex and all the flowing ease of the man.

After 10 overs, at 40 for 1, Imran gives way to Spencer, who bowls off a shortish run for a seamer, with a final stamping of feet like a draught horse coming out of a brewery yard. Arnold is displaced by Cheatle, who twirls down spin. Almost at once the batsmen get into an awful mix-up over a run, from which a stranded Richards only just reaches sanctuary in time. Perhaps Rose is undermined by that alarm, because until now he has played the steady captain's part, not allowing himself to be drawn into recklessness by the simplicity with which he collected those first 14 runs; but now he is caught off the very next ball, from the only false stroke he has made. It is from this point, 53 for 2, that Somerset's supporters are silenced for the first time since the innings began. It becomes apparent that Viv Richards may not give a virtuoso's flashing performance today, that these two bowlers are quietly and persistently beginning to bottle Somerset up. The silence, indeed, is remarkable as Spencer and Cheatle in turn come up to bowl, while nearly 30,000 people wait and stare without a word. It would be oppressive, eerie, if it lasted longer than it takes for a ball to be bowled. It ends with a gasp or a groan or (not too often now) a muted cheer, as the batsman makes his move. The anxiety and urgency is pent up once more and the silence falls again.

Almost palpably, it is having as much effect on the batsmen as anything the bowlers are doing out there. Richards, who is seen at his best when a cricket ground echoes with a cackling joy that he has inspired, is fretting under the curb. He leaps to meet Cheatle's spin, restive to break bonds, and nearly gets himself stumped. But it is Roebuck's overstretched nerve that gives Sussex another advance when he tries to drive a slow full toss, gets under it and gives mid-off a catch.

So Botham comes out on the stroke of noon as if he is about to make someone pay, which is the way he usually comes to bat. His supporters here have mixed feelings about Botham's belligerence in good times and bad. When he goes for Cheatle from the outset they are on their feet cheering, but by the time they sit down they are sucking their teeth in anxiety at the risk. He slams the bowler into the Grandstand for 6, which has bells and bugles sounding round the ground, and a man in front of me waving his plastic bonnet (supplied by Bidgood and Steele, of Bridgwater) in the air. The next ball is defensively blocked and that chap lets out a sigh of relief. "Good boy," he says, blowing out his cheeks, "'E can do it if 'e just takes 'is time." The onus of victory, notice, is implicitly shifted from Viv Richards now. Though hitting the ball beautifully when he can, the world's most exciting batsman is still uncommonly confined. In twenty-five minutes after noon, Somerset's score advances by 40 runs and 24 of these are from Botham's bat, including another 6 off Cheatle. But for his arrival, the scoring rate would be anaemic by the canons of the limited-overs game; as it is, even with that spurt, Somerset are not averaging 4 an over, and hot favourites should be doing better than that.

Then, shortly before lunch, Sussex strike the blow West Country men feared before the match began. Having contained Richards marvellously well in the full quota of overs from Spencer and Cheatle, they get him with an enforced bowling change. Spencer's statutory dozen being done, Barclay's off-spin is brought on at the pavilion end. Richards is encouraged to attack in Botham's wake and sweeps Barclay a couple of times for 4. Nonchalantly, with all the ease in the world, he hauls another ball high into the air, and down on the long-leg boundary Geoff Arnold in a sunhat begins to stir. He moves forward quite slowly, so that his sunhat stays put, while that ball seems to hang in the sky before starting to dip. I hear the rosy lady murmur "Oh, no!" but I am transfixed by Arnold's now stuttering feet, and the arms that are shaping up in front of his face. The yell that goes up when he has the ball and holds it to his chest, splits Lord's asunder in triumph and dismay. The entire Sussex team race over to Arnold and smother him with delight. They have returned to their places and Arnold is back on the ropes, hugging his sides and wrinkling his nose with pleasure, before pandemonium dies down. All Somerset, as well as the bookies, banked on a Richards century today and Sussex are overjoyed to have got him for 44. It is all up to Botham when Somerset go in with 129 for 4 at lunch.

I don't think it is in his nature to be rattled by disaster when he has a bat in his hands; to be injudicious, yes, but not to change whatever was his original course. He was thumping the bowlers when he went in; he continues to belt them when he comes out. His third 6, pulled into the Grandstand off Arnold, is a shot not many would have attempted with their ham salad still going down. He was also very carefully selecting which balls to hit, which ones to leave alone or simply parry before lunch, and he does not abandon this policy after the break. He plays the responsible innings for which my bonneted neighbour had hoped, without the slightest trace of fret. If he had someone to keep him company out there and score at half his rate, Somerset could yet build a total that Sussex would find it hard to pass. Imperiously he waves for an adjustment to the pavilion sightscreen when Imran bowls again, and arrogantly he smashes the Pakistani to the pavilion rails to bring his half century up. This is not enough for the Somerset crowd, with that overall scoring rate on their minds. They shout for acceleration and, in trying to provide it, Marks impatiently lofts Barclay to deep mid-off where, for the second time today, Geoff Arnold sweats the blood of innocence until the ball is safely in his hands.

He is not the greatest fieldsman in county cricket, but he has picked the right moments to surpass himself. Another half dozen runs and Botham sweeps but does not middle the ball, which has merely trickled past square leg. He is still contorted on the ground in the completion of the stroke when Burgess, afflicted by blind hope, comes charging down the pitch and is halfway to Botham when Cheatle starts to throw the ball. Like an elephant trying to turn on a halfpenny, the cumbersome Burgess makes to retreat; but he never has a chance and Somerset are 157 for 6.

Worse, much worse, is the fact that 50 overs are spent for only 160 runs. "Ten overs to score another hundred," says a Somerset fan with a gloomy shake of the head, sensing that his side will do well to achieve half that ambition before the innings must close. Taylor, who followed Burgess to the crease, has performed useful rearguard actions before now, but the galloping requirements of limited-overs cricket are not his strong suit, certainly not against a captain as shrewd as Arnold Long. Knowing very well that everything depends on Botham, the Sussex wicketkeeper, with those ten overs to go, reorganises his field and puts six men on the boundary. If the all-rounder continues to hit for the ropes, he risks being caught and Somerset may then be done for on the cheap. There is an agonised moment early on, when Botham hooks Arnold high above square leg: Javed turns and runs desperately, clutches at the ball as it comes over his shoulder, then drops what would have been a tremendous catch. After that, Botham opts for staying there and collecting ones and twos. For this strategy to succeed he needs a partner with reflexes on edge, a sprinter's speed and a will to be bold. Taylor has none of these things; just an unfortunate knack of taking a single from the end of an over and keeping most of the bowling unprofitably to himself. He'd be too slow for his own funeral, the way he's batting today, and Somerset folk around me say darkly that Rose should have sent Garner to partner Botham instead. The score creeps upwards and those overs seep away. At 194, with scarcely more than a dozen balls of the innings left,

161

Botham lashes defiantly at Imran and has his wicket shattered. His 80 runs have been the backbone of Somerset
this afternoon, but they should have been fleshed out by
somebody else. Garner gives a hint of what might have
been, with 8 runs in the last 2 overs, where Taylor has
made only 13 in 12, when the batsmen come in at 207 for
7.

This is the only time since 1973 that the side batting first
in the Cup Final has reached 200 runs, and in itself the
score can hardly account for the lowered spirits of the
Somerset supporters. The smocks and the crooks are no
longer jiggling buoyantly down on the grass by the boundary ropes, and in the Mound Stand my neighbours are
talking of the match as touch and go, when they had
expected something much more decisive at the halfway
stage. When their own side came to bat they were brist-
ling in anticipation of the booty ahead. At Sussex's turn
they are clenched in suspense on the edge of their seats.
Only a few murmurs are heard when Garner bowls an
opening maiden to Barclay, his massive body tilted forward with hands almost touching in attitude of prayer as
he begins his run-up, like a high jumper breaking into his
stride in the rhythmic concentration of his approach. His
pounding feet are enough to shake the earth, requiring
much courage in a batsman merely to stand and wait for
the ball to fly from that remarkable height. I do not think
many will have the nerve to hit at Garner's first deliveries
with a gleaming new ball. It is sufficient to get behind
them and stun them dead, as Barclay does a couple,
thankful that the rest can be observed for future reference
as they go flashing past the off-stump. Dredge comes up
in jerking bounds to start his work from the Nursery end
and Mendis turns the ball sharply off his feet, sees it go
directly to Jennings at square leg, straight into his cupped
hands so that he doesn't have to move an inch. A roar
from all Somerset, their players leaping upwards in
delight; all but poor Jennings, who is looking at the
ground where the ball has spilled.

Two overs without score is no compensation for that.
Nor is the added pressure on Barclay in Garner's second

over, when Richards thinks he has a catch off bat, not pad, and flings the ball high in excitement. Maybe it is this second frustration that undoes the West Country men now, persuading the batsmen that if they have survived such a torrid start there is little they cannot do if they try. Gradually they bring attacking strokes to bear, and after 10 overs have seen both opening bowlers off for 35 runs. In the next over, with Botham bowling, they have caught up with Somerset's scoring rate, but nearly lose a wicket when they try a second run. Dredge's throw goes to Taylor all right, but the keeper drops the ball with Barclay still yards from the crease. As the score passes the half century, for the first time in this match the Sussex supporters put their weight behind their team. They haven't come to Lord's in fancy dress, so they are not nearly as visible as so many of the coachloads from Taunton way, and Sussex rosettes are sprinkled quite thinly round the ground, almost lost among the thick clusters from the West. Their shouts, when play has gone their way so far, have been aggressive enough, but lacking the deep volume that suggests absolute conviction in its cause. But now they have seen Mendis and Barclay carefully making way, not batting dramatically, not startling the crowd with any one superlative stroke; just cultivating runs and steadily getting on top. So, above the babble of the stands, "Good old Sussex by the sea" surges up in gathering waves. By the time their openers have reached 90, with only just over a third of their overs done, the Sussex crowd have much to sing about. At the same stage this morning, Somerset were only 66 for 2. Rose has tried the high pace of Garner, Botham and Dredge, the persevering seam of Jennings and Burgess, and nothing has come off. A hint of anguish slips into Somerset's play. Taylor appeals for a stumping of Barclay and, when Dickie Bird turns it down, the keeper flings the ball to the ground.

At 93, just before tea, Somerset at last get a break when Mendis drives at Burgess and slices the ball to Marks at short third man. But it is after the interval that drama returns to the match for the first time since the opening overs of the Sussex innings. First, Barclay's patient foundation is dislodged when he hooks at Botham's bouncer and skies the ball to Roebuck at mid-wicket. Without another run added, Javed flicks at Garner; and Taylor, flinging himself full-length to his right, takes the ball just before it touches the ground and redeems almost everything he has done wrong in the match so far. Now Somerset's damped fires flare up again and, with Imran scarcely begun, Botham lets another bouncer loose. The batsman just manages to get his skull out of the way, the ball whipping off his cap as he bends hurriedly at the knees. But Botham has done the damage he wanted to inflict. As he walks back to his mark, Imran is still giving his head a bit of a rub, where imagination tells him the sniper's bullet just missed. Botham bowls again, full length this time, and Imran, with the spasm of a frightened man, holds his bat in front of him, somewhere between the heavens and hell. The ball rebounds upwards and Botham rushes on frantically to grab it before it reaches the ground. Sussex have just lost 3 wickets in nine deliveries for only 4 runs. What was 93 for 0 has become 110 for 4.

Western spirits rise again and "Sussex by the sea" ebbs away. Another break-through now and the notoriously long batting tail will be laid bare. For a dozen or so overs after coming together, Parker and Phillipson go very gingerly indeed, the weight of their responsibilities bowing them in concentrated defence. Between the twenty-eighth over, when that fourth wicket fell, and the forty-first, only 33 runs are scored; but what matters most in that period is the batsmen's endurance, not the slackening flow of runs. Rose has again put everything available into his attack, has himself patrolled the midfield keenly, as sentry, scout and commander embodied in one. From there he has watched the gradual spiking of his guns. The looser balls become more frequent and Parker drives many of them to the covers with a style and confidence that, by the end of the day, will have people in this crowd wondering whether they have perhaps seen another young man with the potential of Botham and Gower. Botham, in fact, does badly this evening. Finding the craft of ballistics thwarted by Parker's skill, he tries to compensate with increased aggression and in 2 overs yields 16 runs which include a couple of wides and a brace of no-balls. My neighbour from Bridgwater takes Bidgood and Steele's bonnet from his head and fans his face in despair, muttering that Botham always turns up trumps for England, but never for his county; which is a bit unjust, but contains a little truth.

From the forty-second over, Sussex move ahead of Somerset's scoring rate more emphatically with every salvo bowled. As the occasional cloud is unravelled across the blue sky above Lord's, Parker and Phillipson go purposefully on, while the Sussex singing begins again and swells. As the 200 goes up with 10 overs still to come and 6 wickets still to fall, Somerset's men move with resignation about the field. They know that a miracle will not now intervene. The scores are levelled and Phillipson, the dogged liegeman, Martin Lightfoot to Hereward the Wake, tries to hit the winning run off Dredge. He only nicks the ball and is caught behind. So Parker strikes the blow off Denning, who is brought up symbolically to surrender Somerset's sword. It has not been the most exciting Cup Final by any means, lacking terminal suspense to qualify for that. But it has been a very famous victory for the underdogs, who had seemed so ill-equipped to take a trophy they were the first to win in 1963. As the old chap said, Viv Richards was only human after all. Parker is declared Man of the Match, and Somerset folk don't linger to see him collect his £100, his gold medal and his special necktie for the feat. Before the presentation starts, the roads outside Lord's are full of refugees heading West. Young men brandish pieces of cardboard indicating "Taunton" in the traffic's face, and look worried at what the morrow might bring.

### SOMERSET

| | |
|---|---|
| B. C. ROSE c Long b Cheatle | 30 |
| P. A. DENNING b Imran | 0 |
| I. V. A. RICHARDS c Arnold b Barclay | 44 |

| | |
|---|---:|
| P. M. ROEBUCK c Mendis b Cheatle | 9 |
| I. T. BOTHAM b Imran | 80 |
| V. J. MARKS c Arnold b Barclay | 4 |
| G. I. BURGESS run out | 3 |
| D. J. S. TAYLOR not out | 13 |
| J. GARNER not out | 8 |
| Extras (lb 10, nb 6) | 16 |
| | |
| Total (for 7, 60 overs) | 207 |

Fall of wickets: 22, 53, 73, 115, 151, 157, 194.
Did not bat: K. F. Jennings, C. F. Dredge.
Bowling: IMRAN 12–1–50–2; ARNOLD 12–2–43–0; SPENCER 12–3–27–0; CHEATLE 12–3–50–2; BARCLAY 12–3–21–2.

## SUSSEX

| | |
|---|---:|
| J. R. T BARCLAY c Roebuck b Botham | 44 |
| G. D. MENDIS c Marks b Burgess | 44 |
| P. W. G. PARKER not out | 62 |
| JAVED MIANDAD c Taylor b Garner | 0 |
| IMRAN KHAN c and b Botham | 3 |
| C. P. PHILLIPSON c Taylor b Dredge | 32 |
| S. J. STOREY not out | 0 |
| Extras (b 1, lb 9, w 7, nb 9) | 26 |
| | |
| Total (for 5, 53.1 overs) | 211 |

Fall of wickets: 93, 106, 106, 110, 207.
Did not bat: A. A. Long, J. Spencer, G. G. Arnold, R. G. L. Cheatle.
Bowling: GARNER 12–3–34–1; DREDGE 10–2–26–1; BOTHAM 12–1–65–2; JENNINGS 9–1–29–0; BURGESS 10–2–27–1; DENNING 0.1–0–4–0.
Umpires: H. D. Bird and B. J. Meyer.
Sussex beat Somerset by 5 wickets.

# The Hambledon Game

*September 3*                    *Broadhalfpenny Down*
**BRIGANDS v HAMBLEDON**

THE FIELD SLOPES AWAY FROM CROSS-ROADS ON TOP OF A ridge. One side is lined by beech trees, which conceal the road running to Hambledon village a couple of miles away. At the junction stands the Bat and Ball Inn, white-washed on its lower courses at the front, otherwise pink-pantiled overall. It is quite a small alehouse, the sort that may have seen highwaymen on portentously stormy nights, when inn signs creak and swing. From the taproom windows on this warm late summer's afternoon, you can look across the narrow road and the low hedge on the other side, to where cricketers are playing on that field of Broadhalfpenny Down. Because the slope falls gently from the inn and over the field before taking a steeper plunge, it seems as if the far boundary might slip off into the sky, but the fertile land of Hampshire rolls away in a patchwork of gold and green beyond. You can hear pheasants clacking in coverts nearby, and the clop of a riding school along the Hambledon road. This is comforting when the inn and the cricket field, the cross-roads and the line of trees are rather lonely by themselves. A stumpy granite monument by the gate leading into the field suggests some corner of the Highlands made desolate by Passchendaele and the Somme, but has a fruitful significance to tell. In spite of Lord and all his works, this is the most precious piece of earth known to the best-loved game. It is not the birthplace of cricket, which will be some anonymous sheep pasture on the Weald of Kent, but the place where, as John Arlott has written, the local club "was the first in the history of cricket both to achieve major success, and to be adequately chronicled."

It is the Brigands who occupy this heirloom from the

Nyrens and their peers, while today's Hambledon men play their home games on a much younger ground by the village. Broadhalfpenny Down, ploughed under by Victorians and restored to cricket forever by Winchester College in 1924, is let for a peppercorn rent to the sailors of HMS *Mercury*, whose aerials and topmast rise above trees on another ridge to the north. That is where My Lords Commissioners once taught me how to decode their messages, which frequently baffled me even when I'd done, and where the Brigands spend their non-playing days in similar pursuits. They should, I think, have run the White Ensign up the pavilion flagstaff this afternoon, for their captain is ticking off one of his latecomers as though quarter-deck and not sacred turf were underneath his feet.

That pavilion, as it happens, has provided the excuse for a fine old gesture to the past. Its thatch is wearing thin and other parts also need repair. So the Hambledon men have made a helpful challenge, with wagers on the result. If the sailors win this match, the Hambledon club will find £25 towards the workmen's bill; if the villagers triumph, they will tip up only £10. This is not on the scale that eighteenth-century Hambledon knew, when Richard Nyren would lead his team against All England for purses of up to 2,000 guineas and side stakes as well, but it will do for these chapfallen times. In Richard's old pub across the road, they have framed the scorecard of the most cele-brated victory of the Hambledon men, who won twenty-nine matches against England between 1772 and 1781. In a fixture beginning on June 18, 1777, they scored 403 runs in one innings and dismissed All England for 166 and 69; and there are all the details, tricked out with curli-cues and a flourished title at the top. For three decades those village cricketers attracted the best players, the biggest patrons and thousands of spectators to their games on Broadhalfpenny and, later, on Windmill Down. After that, the lustre passed to the Marylebone Club, and much of cricket's profit was made in the capital by the speculating Thomas Lord. But enchantment can never be taken from this place.

When the sailors start batting this afternoon maybe two dozen people have come to watch, and a couple of ladies are keeping score. They do this in the old-fashioned way, not putting initials to anyone's name. Dogs abound, including our Sam, who shamed me terribly before anyone else turned up by desecrating Broadhalfpenny in the region of third man. The cricketers have quite enough to beware of out there without that. Although the whole field has been mown so sweetly as to leave a velvet nap to the very edge, moles have ringed the lower boundary with piles of earth and the grass is stippled with fragments of chalky flint. Hazards and all, it is a healing place on a day like this, with cabbage whites fluttering in the sun, and the sound of the Bat and Ball's front door swinging to as someone else comes out with a drink in his hand. Everyone lingers in there for a while. Its low taproom cannot have changed much since Richard kept the inn, and they have his old bat clamped into brackets above the bar; a heavy piece of timber, curved in the eighteenth-century manner and made, probably by John Small, for cudgelling runs. A picture of John Nyren, chronicler of Hambledon in cricket's first classic writing, hangs by the inglenook alongside a portrait of Silver Billy Beldham who, according to John, was the finest batter of his age and "as safe as the Bank". No one, thank heaven, has lifted a finger to tart the room up. It is still benches and long tables and dark panelling round the walls. A few horse brasses on the beams is the worst that progress has done.

And the sailors, I see, have a taste for things past, with adhesive tape binding the most fashionable new bats. With these they are soon breezing along against the Hambledon men at a fair rate of knots. By the time Sabbath licensing closes the Bat and Ball's door, they have made 70 for 1 inside an hour and several healthy boundaries have been struck down the slope. Fielders obligingly signal the ball's crossing of the line, which is invisible to any umpire not standing on a chair. One straight drive all but carries for 6 into the sightscreen in front of the beech trees; had it done so, there might have been need for further repairs. As it is, the sightscreen's canvas hangs torn and loose, from which I assume that sailmakers are in short supply in my old ship; or possibly have been dispensed with in the electrified Navy of today. Some things, however, are as they always were. The Brigands' captain comes in to bat when the second wicket falls at 94, looks impressive for a couple of overs, then gets a brutal knock on the funny bone. Two Hambledon players help him back to the pavilion, where other Brigands have been watching sympathetically from deckchairs. As their captain comes aboard they rise as one man, form flanks and escort him solicitously inside. This reflex belongs to a drill movement on the Queen's Birthday Parade, and if they keep on like that I imagine they'll do pretty well in their chosen careers.

For a little while longer the naval innings holds its course, and the Hambledon men strive to end the defiance of Number Three, whose half century is beginning to come into his line of fire. A donkey brays somewhere across the Hambledon road and, every now and then, the isolated sounds of cricket break through a hidden disturbance of ducks or geese. The afternoon is heavy with contentment and warmth; peaceful, soothing and, without the movement of players, utterly still. Half the spectators seem to be dozing where they lie sprawled upon the grass. The rest of us, except for those waiting to bat, are not intent upon the technicalities of the game. One does not need to be to enjoy cricket on an idyllic summer's day. It is enough to absorb dreamily the aesthetic of the scene, the graceful movement, the contrast between colours, between light and shade, the sense of careful order going on and on. The truth is that one is watching this match with only half an eye, that these players are perceived through a recollection of the past, and that they bear only hereditary resemblance to the Hambledon men of old.

Two centuries ago, Broadhalfpenny did not tremble with figures in luminous white. Richard Nyren's team wore sky-blue coats with black velvet collars, and silver-laced hats when they were in Lord Winchilsea's pay. They appeared in silk breeches, long stockings and buckled shoes, and their legs were not protected from the ball by anything but their hose. Beldham said that you would see a bump heave under the stocking and then the blood come through; and he remembered John Wells, who was built like a cob-horse and was a baker by trade, tearing off a finger nail against his shoe buckle when bending to pick up a ball. The Bat and Ball's brewers have pictured them more or less as they were. On one side of the inn sign is a portrait of John Nyren, who immortalised that team. On the other a batsman is about to strike with something not much different from a hockey stick, and the wicketkeeper crouches behind a kind of croquet hoop. That would be before Lumpy Stevens of All England bowled three balls clean through John Small's wicket without disturbing the bails, which led to the introduction of the middle stump they're playing with today.

Number Three doesn't get his half century. He is removed by Hambledon's second change bowler, who has already done damage to the Brigands with his high delivery and good length. John Nyren speaks of Barber and Hogsflesh taking their wickets in this style (though they were bowling underarm) and either would have been happy to return Barrett's figures this afternoon. The sailors sink from 127 for 3 to a declaration at 177 for 8 and Barrett comes in with five of those wickets for only 32 runs. He flops on the grass by the pavilion, with two or three other Hambledon men and a couple of their wives, while the sailors tap the tea urn and hand round cucumber sandwiches, and the ladies who have kept score get up and stretch their legs. There are perhaps fifty spectators on Broadhalfpenny by now, and cars stand in line abreast along the length of the hedge inside the field. No one is shouting odds on the result of this wager match, though one sailor informs another that he picked up ten quid on Sussex's victory at Lord's yesterday.

Not a cry is heard from any watcher when Hambledon come to bat, nor is there more than a token clap when they lose an early wicket, then another on the cheap. Conceivably everyone else is as riveted as I am by the

171

dazzling headgear of the Brigands, who have transformed the cricket match from a neat into a gaudy thing. When Hambledon were in the field there was one sunhat and ten bare heads, but the sailors have gone overboard in dressing the ship. Every colour in the spectrum stripes those caps fore and aft, in half a dozen club combinations between the eleven men. It occurs to me that such a display is a subtle ploy, for a batsman could well be cross-eyed after looking quickly round before shaping up to the next ball. If so, it fails completely once those two wickets have gone for 37. The Hambledon men begin to knock the ball to all quarters of Broadhalfpenny, aided by the introduction of a bowler whose deliveries come so slowly through the air that, even from the shade of the beech trees, it is possible to believe that you can see the stitching on the seam. As the batsmen gallop their singles, their twos and sometimes their threes, I listen for Hampshire voices shouting "Go hard! Go hard! *Tich* and turn! *Tich* and turn!" But there is no sound except that of thumping feet and, behind me, of wood pigeons canoodling in the trees. In the lee of a car, a woman continues with what she has been doing ever since her husband disembarked to go and play. Her eyes have rarely strayed from her needles, which are knitting socks of navy blue.

Hambledon's third wicket falls at 97, but after that there is no joy for the Brigands until the Bat and Ball's door is reopened with a snapping of latches and a squeaking of the hinge, and the villagers are within sight of the winning runs. The sun has turned from a glaring white to a glowing red and an evening haze softens all light on the folded land. Down in the bottom, below Broadhalfpenny, a combine harvester stands beside a large strawstack at its Sunday rest. Was that the field where John Small pacified the bull with his double bass? A man of many parts, he was, a cobbler in Petersfield whose shop sign said:

> Here lives John Small
> Makes bat and ball
> Pitch a wicket, play at cricket
> With any man in England.

172

He was, as well, the best short runner of his day; and a good fiddler, to boot, who taught himself to play the double bass. Nyren tells how he had to cross two or three fields on his way to a musical party and was attacked by the bull; "when our hero, with the characteristic coolness and presence of mind of a good cricketer, began playing upon his bass, to the admiration and perfect satisfaction of the mischievous beast." Was that the field, where the combine now stands? Or was it just over that hedge, where the stubble has already been burnt? Or further up the slope, in that vivid crop of mustard? Or was it in some field miles away, much nearer Petersfield? It doesn't really matter when, like John Small's accomplishments, it's all of a piece.

We do not stay to see the end of the game, because there are four counties to cross before Sam and we get home, and I've promised Herself that we'll take in Tichborne on the way, and some watercress beds along the valley of the Test. Hambledon are going well when we leave Broadhalfpenny Down and later I hear that they have won the challenge match by 5 wickets. They settled that wager, of course, in the building by the cross-roads, where their ancestors gathered on match days, as well as for club meetings and an annual dinner. I hope that when the purse was set aside, enough was left in the kitty for drinks all round, and that the Hambledon men did not forget to toast the Immortal Memory of Madge.

### BRIGANDS

| | |
|---|---:|
| NEWMAN lbw Barrett | 58 |
| FREEMAN c Tomkins b Horn | 15 |
| BANES-WALKER c and b Barrett | 42 |
| MARSHALL retired hurt | 8 |
| ASHENDEN b Barrett | 7 |
| BAZALGETTE run out | 10 |
| COLLINS c Stevenson b Barrett | 5 |
| WOOD b Barrett | 9 |

| | |
|---|---|
| HEALEY b Stevenson | 11 |
| ELLIS not out | 3 |
| Extras | 9 |
| | —— |
| Total (for 8, declared) | 177 |

Fall of wickets: 20, 94, 127, 137, 148, 150, 173, 177.
Did not bat: Mackay.
Bowling: HORN 6–0–30–1; STEVENSON 13.5–3–42–1; TURNER 15–1–64–0; BARRETT 18–3–32–5.

## HAMBLEDON

| | |
|---|---|
| TURNER c Freeman b Healey | 64 |
| MCGRATH b Ellis | 3 |
| TOMKINS c Marshall b Ashenden | 8 |
| WINGHAM lbw Collins | 32 |
| LUTYENS b Bazalgette | 56 |
| HORN not out | 10 |
| BARRETT not out | 4 |
| Extras | 2 |
| | —— |
| Total (for 5) | 179 |

Fall of wickets: 5, 37, 97, 159, 168.
Did not bat: Hughes, Enstone, Stevenson and Miller.
Bowling: HEALEY 13–1–50–1; ELLIS 10–1–32–1; ASHENDEN 6–1–29–1; COLLINS 5–0–28–1; MARSHALL 2–0–23–0; BAZALGETTE 5–1–17–1.
Umpires: Sims and Rock.
Hambledon beat Brigands by 5 wickets.

# Close of Play

IT WASN'T HARD TO DECIDE WHERE THE LAST DAYS OF THE
season should be spent. Of all the major grounds, Trent
Bridge arouses the widest and deepest affection among
strangers, whether they are playing in a Test match or
simply watching a county game. It has managed to
achieve the perfect balance between a stadium and a less
ambitious cricket ground where players and watchers are
blended into one. It is palatial compared with the Oval or
Headingley, but it lacks the studied grandeur of Lord's,
has more charm than Old Trafford and is instinct with
history that has eluded Edgbaston so far. Neville Cardus
called it "a place where it was always afternoon and 360
for 2 wickets", which said something for the blessed
mood of Trent Bridge as well as the blandness of its turf. It
is still the ground that brings the nearest thing to a sparkle
into Boycott's calculating eye, and that pitch may have
tipped the balance in Ray Illingworth's choice of a future
with Leicester rather than Notts. Above all, though, Trent
Bridge is where you feel emotionally bound to the fine
arts and mellowed growth of this game at its civilising
best. You can be sustained through much more than a
winter on a memory of cricket in this place.

Another reason for coming is that this might have been
a match to decide the county championship if Essex
hadn't been plagued by atrocious weather over the final
stretch. They reach their last game as runners-up to Kent,
in spite of having lost only one three-day contest this
year, whereas the champions have already been beaten
twice. It has been a perfect season on the land, whatever
the farmers may subsequently plead, but cricket needs

175

different weather from what is ideal for crops. This side of England is lurid now with flames blazing across fields every night, as the stubble is burned off with the harvest done. As I drove up the Great North Road, the headlands of Lincolnshire were already being harrowed for winter seed, under windy skies that kept flocks of cloud running away from the sun, and gulls banking tipsily in the tractor's wake. The great cooling towers at Ratcliffe-on-Soar were a row of volcanoes pluming their vapours into a heavenly blue, and Nottingham itself gleamed with freshness in the mid-morning light. Yet the day was deceptively fine for cricket, and Essex have brought with them their recent rotten luck. There was a deluge in the night and the outfield waters have not nearly subsided by the time play should have started at half past eleven. One day, I suppose, administrators will solve the problem of rain-affected grounds, so that we shall be spared having to wait hours for them to be fit for a game. Meanwhile, we watch six acres at Trent Bridge slowly drying out, while the groundsmen shift their drainage tackle here and there.

Few people have turned up and I don't meet a soul behind the Bridgford Road stands, when I look for the patch of concrete where George Parr's elm tree stood until it was uprooted in a gale two years ago. As lunch-time approaches, there is an influx of expense accounters making for the restaurant beside the pavilion where, on top of the avocado and the escalope de veau, they should be enjoying a clear view of cricket within a few feet of the grass. They're very strong on catering at Trent Bridge, and not only as a means of keeping the county club financially afloat. In a shack behind the pavilion you can obtain in great comfort the best sandwiches I have ever tasted at a cricket match, with the cheese and onion, or what you will, almost too much for the halves of freshly-baked bread. I hope the players are served as well, behind that balcony where baskets of flowers hang. The only sight of them this morning has been of Gooch and Denness, returning to their dressing room in track suits, hot from squash. It is on such brief visions that we cricket-watchers feed enough to endure the tedium of the waiting game.

At last, at twenty to four, the most impressive score-board in English cricket flicks into action with the same pattering of names and figures that we see on all the best railway stations when trains are announced. And at least the long vigil has not been for a dull grafting in the dwindling day. Notts lose one of their openers almost as soon as they come to bat; which means that we enjoy two hours of Derek Randall at his jauntiest, full of zest. After a season of not being picked for a single Test, he has just got the nod for the Australian tour and bats this evening like a man with a load off his mind. His critics, naturally, argue that he is always a mite too carefree for the stern responsibilities of the international scene, quite apart from the matter of his two-eyed stance, which makes them wonder whether Randall thinks he's playing French cricket on a seaside beach. I think they are too much irritated by his total inability to be still even when he's facing bowlers who turn some men to stone. I'll swear that at every ball he receives this evening, he first tugs at his sweater and readjusts his box before going into his fidgety version of settling down.

He is much more effective than Fletcher could have wished when he asked the home side to take the first knock. In spite of moving across his stumps before the ball has left the bowler's hand, his driving and hooking are perfectly timed and, though he does not score at break-neck speed, he doesn't for a moment suggest that he won't get the runs. John Lever's blond hair is already wet with hard work when he holds one back to trick this impish man; but Randall jerks to a standstill on his way to somewhere else, regains a sort of balance, and drives the slower ball square through the covers for 4. The next one is a yorker, which he comes down on just in time. He grins with the pleasure of still being there, then shakes an amiable fist at his fellow tourist, which is not returned but makes Trent Bridge glow with fondness for its favourite son. In Turner's fifth over, two successive balls are put over the ropes, with a drive and a hook, exactly opposite each other to Randall's right and left. Down at long leg,

Ray East sits on a bench among the spectators while Turner is walking back to his mark. It's been a long season for him, with all the chores of his benefit to perform, and he could do with taking the weight off when Todd and Randall are not making him run about. Todd bats sturdily while Randall catches the eye so that, even when he's not scoring, the time seems to skate past. It doesn't feel as though we've been watching for a couple of hours when he scampers 3, like a puppy chasing a ball with its limbs all but tripping it up, to reach half a century just before close of play.

Another downpour overnight delays the start of the second day until half past two but, four hours before that, Randall is puffing round the field in his track suit, his beaky face screwed into creases that, even at its happy-go-luckiest, are liable to give it an anxious air. Then he does some exercises at the Ratcliffe Road end, touching toes, beating his chest, lying full-length and jack-knifing up. Two or three motherly souls watch him from afar, one of them having arrived with two generations of her family in tow, laden with thermos flasks and eatables, keen to secure good seats in the almost empty stand.

"I used to play in the Guides, believe it or not," she's telling the youngsters as they spread themselves out. She hails another woman, sitting by herself twenty yards away. "I've just been saying to my grandsons, cricket teaches you patience."

The other nods to the figure of Randall, distantly flexing his back. "Oh, I don't mind that," she says. "I'm more worried about Derek lying on that damp ground." He comes past a bit later, on his way to the dressing room, the track suit smeared with mud. "Eh, Derek," she says, "you want to see your back. It's a proper mess."

He cocks a cheeky head, the lad who knows he's too old to get a clip on the ear. "They're not mine," he says. "They're Trevor Tunnicliffe's and I haven't told him yet."

Before play starts this afternoon, he has boys from the small crowd bowling to him below the pavilion seats. He's a very natural man, and Trent Bridge encourages good nature between those who play and those who watch. In the whole of this great ground they are separated by only twenty yards of fence in front of those seats. Rice and Gooch, McEwan and Todd are also practising there; and not a ball is tossed back to them from the watchers without a "thanks" from the cricketers and a genuine smile.

From 92 for 1, Notts reach 140 before another wicket falls. Fletcher brings up his spinners early on the drying pitch and, at first, Todd and Randall carry on in much the same way as they were batting last night. But as the ball starts to turn more from Acfield and East, the batsmen begin to be lucky with some of their shots. Randall has more than his fair share of fortune when he swings at one ball from East and gets a single off the thinnest edge. As he rushes to the other end, his bright blue Nottinghamshire cap falls off and East takes a stiff-legged punt at it on the ground. Maybe his patience is wearing thin, though it's hard to tell; with Randall himself, East is cricket's most notable jester, but droll, where Randall is pert. A little later he goes into one of his favourite routines to indicate despair, picking up a handful of sawdust and making it seem to trickle out of his head; at which Umpire Oslear doubles up more than usual over the stumps in mirth. East has the last laugh on Randall today, when another swing and another edge swirl the ball to Gooch at cover point. But those 86 runs have been good to watch.

Rice comes in, and Notts will be very thankful that his differences with the club were smoothed away so quickly at the beginning of the year. He ends this season with the best batting average in the land, more than 11 runs ahead of Glenn Turner's figure, and without him the county could hardly have risen from the bottom of the championship, ten places to seventh. I don't know how much of his success may be attributed to his stance, but it is the antithesis of the way Randall shapes up to bat. Rice crouches sideways on to the bowler, knock-kneed as a golfer preparing to putt, with the same meticulous concentration and slightly cramped arms; until the ball takes flight, when he is upright, with his bat off the ground and his feet moving fast. His average suffers today, though, just as he is beginning to strike out, when he tries to play Acfield off his legs and is caught at forward short leg. The catch is taken by Hardie who, five runs before, had a hand in finishing Todd's increasingly laborious innings. I mention Hardie only because, for the first time since the Test match in June, I have been subjected to the spectacle of a crash-helmeted cricketer again. Until he moved in close just before dismissing Rice, Hardie had been nowhere nearer the batsmen than square leg since play began yesterday. He had been wandering round the mid-field with his visor pointing up to the sky, the image of a child refusing to be separated from its new Christmas toy, in this case something that belongs to the current instalment of "Dr Who". I hope that before next season starts, he will remove the thing long enough for someone to have a word in his ludicrously sheltered ear.

After Rice goes, at 172 for 4, the spin bowling becomes altogether too much for Notts and wickets fall in short order, with just enough resistance from Mackintosh to secure a second batting point at 200 for 8. Then Smedley declares and, when Essex start to bat, hedges his attacking bets with Cooper's seam at one end, Doshi's spin at the other. This takes out Gooch before the first over is done, pushing at Cooper and caught in the slips. But Lilley and McEwan, after watching the bowlers carefully for a while, begin to attack with such effect that Randall is soon doing his midfield gymnastics to cut off balls that most men would never nearly approach. When he comes in this evening his flannels are slutched up from the ankles to the hip, with all the frantic sliding he has done across the tacky ground. He has probably saved Notts a dozen runs with those goalkeeping dives; as it is, Essex reach 50 without further loss. Then Doshi's spin bamboozles Lilley into slipping a catch to Rice; and, minutes later, a drive by McEwan off the Indian is held low down by Cooper, imitating Randall at mid-off. When play ends, Essex are 55 for 3 but, with two more innings to come when this one is done, the match seems destined for some kind of draw.

The last day of the season starts on time in such brilliant

sunshine that Ken Palmer comes out to umpire in a straw hat. Already there are more people in Trent Bridge than on the other two days put together, and young men sit with their bicycles propped beside them among the slender columns of the Bridgford Road stands. In the small square inside the main gates, between the club offices and a shading tree, the symbols of modest cricketing affluence are parked; cars dished out by motor dealers, so plastered with their advertising that if one passed you on the motorway it would be hard to tell whether there was a county cricketer or a commercial traveller inside. I feel awfully old-fashioned in preferring that serviceable van which simply says "Essex County Cricket Club". On impulse I go into the office and plunge a few quid on a souvenir that will please me for the rest of my life (and I hope the children mind which of them has it after me). When George Parr's elm was blown down, Notts had the timber made into miniature bats nearly a foot long. Mine is Number 857, a perfectly formed and lovely thing that you could run your hands over all day. Gunn and Moore's work, I shouldn't wonder.

It was as well to be here from the start this morning, because Essex lose four wickets within the first half hour. East, the night-watchman, is gone before I'm properly sat down. Then Doshi removes Hardie and Pont with consecutive balls, and in the next over Smedley takes a great diving catch at square leg to get rid of Turner. This miserable 75 for 7 from the runners-up in the county championship so excites an ancient man in the Parr Stand that he bawls "What-a-load-o'-rubbish!" in the same sing-song he'd use if he were seventy years younger and watching football half a mile away on the Forest ground. Then he remembers where he is, and what has happened too often at Trent Bridge for more years than he'd like to think. "Not that it'll do 'ee any good, Notts", he mumbles to himself. "No justice in life. Never were!" The undertones of his grievance dribble out of his corner while Keith Fletcher studiously refuses to give way to the Nottinghamshire bowlers, though contriving to look rather sheepish about what he's doing out there. At the other end Smith begins to bruise the surging pride of Notts by having a go and being lucky enough not to mishit. The two of them hitch the Essex score from the miserable to the mediocre; whereupon Fletcher, at 122 for 7, in his turn declares. That is nothing more than a decency, of course, in a game shortened by too much overnight rain. He can hardly hope for match-winning points at a quarter past noon with two innings to come, even though this wicket is now, under the sun, a splendid one for spinners, and he the captain with the more redoubtable pair.

But Todd, at any rate, looks as though he's going in the direction of a result when Notts bat again, 78 runs ahead before they start. Before one o'clock another 38 runs are on the board, and 29 of them are his. Dexter is not much happier now than he was on Wednesday and, the moment the spin bowling starts, he falls to East. Randall comes and goes in very nearly the same breath, a double triumph for the other joker in the pack. Then Todd is bowled by Acfield and Notts are 43 for 3. Clive Rice is hitting the ball so hard that half a dozen Essex players are left wringing their hands when they have stopped it breaking through the ring. It is twenty minutes before the South African gets his first run, so tightly disciplined is that field, so fine the alliance between the spinners and the rest of Fletcher's men. Their own South African, McEwan, goes one better than just stopping the ball; he springs forward like a buck and Rice is caught off bat and pad for only 3. Essex bend to it again, and do not now act like cricketers who assume this match must end in a draw. Nor do Smedley and young French, who looks even more schoolboyish when batting than when he is upholstered behind the stumps. Nottinghamshire's captain applies himself methodically, as though his best batsmen hadn't just gone for a song, while his wicketkeeper is obdurate and hair-raising in about equal parts. Both enjoy an amount of luck off the pitch, judging by the responses of Acfield and East. Acfield, short and bouncy, groans aloud at his misfortunes from time to time. The tall and rolling East goes in for pantomime. He bowls a maiden to Smedley, a very good one he thinks. He listens dramatically for applause rippling round Trent Bridge. Not a sound except traffic rumbling along Bridgford Road. So he claps loudly himself, and shambles back to his fielding position, shaking a disappointed head.

Notts do not struggle to a declaration at 143 for 5; they get there with as handsome a captain's knock as could be expected on such a day, with spirited assistance from French, who is well caught and bowled by East when driving hard above the spinner's head. Smedley, 48 not out himself, will surely be confident that if his bowlers can't run through Essex a second time today they at least are in small danger of losing the match. The visitors need 222 in 142 minutes and, with the sunshine frequently obscured now by low cloud, it is possible that they might not even have that time to play with. Gooch and Lilley begin steadily, and no more, to the right and left-handed pace of Cooper and Hacker. After such a cascade of wickets as we have seen so far, Essex will be more pleased that the opening partnership is still unbroken at teatime than by the scoring of 50 runs in just under an hour. Gooch, also bound for Australia next month, looks reliable more than commanding. Lilley, in his first county championship match, follows calmly behind. The bowlers fling themselves into their work steadily, too, do not look like separating this pair, but don't offer anything on a plate either. Randall entertains everybody from the covers with some fine cricket and enough comedy to make you smile. He is Walter Mitty this afternoon, taking off on one flight of fancy after another as he waits for the next ball to be bowled. He marches like a soldier to a new position in the field ("Bags o' bull, now, I want ter see those arms *swing!*"). Ten minutes later he's playing the ukelele. Then he's jiving at a Saturday night hop. There is no other sport that would allow a man the time to fit such antics into his game, and probably none that would license them if it could. What Connors and Nastase do are calculated stratagems to help them win a tennis match. What Randall does is no more than an urchin's wish to delight and cast gloom away. I'm not surprised the old ladies of Trent Bridge worry about him catching his death of cold.

183

The moment tea is over, the match is transformed. In ten minutes the batsmen hit 25 runs off Doshi and All-brook, who have replaced the pacemen. Then the players run for shelter as a cloud sprays the ground. In another ten minutes they are back, and a bombardment begins such as I have not seen this season on any cricket field. It starts against growing odds that say Essex cannot possibly win this match: 133 runs are still needed from 20 overs when the last hour's play is marked on the clock. Although he has been trailing Gooch so far, it is the novice Lilley who leads a terrible counter-attack on Allbrook. He pulls the first three balls of the off-spinner's over for 4, 6 and 2, then cuts the fourth down to third man for 3. Gooch hammers the fifth and sixth balls to the boundaries himself – and poor Allbrook is 23 runs the worse for wear. Doshi is much less expensive but he's having trouble with his grip now, needing to wipe the ball dry after almost every delivery. The sun has gone and no longer is this the spinner's wicket of earlier in the day; nor will it be until wind and warmth come to it again. Doshi, fielding on the edge of the ground at long leg, explains to some Notts supporters how the rain has spoiled the match as a contest, tilting it too much the batsmen's way. One old chap isn't having any of that. "D'ye realise they got 25 runs in two overs before t' rain came?" The Indian, polishing his spectacles, is round-eyed with surprise. "Aye," says the old chap, "when you and Allbrook were bowling!" Communion with your spectators isn't always a fortifying thing.

Smedley switches bowlers rapidly, but nothing stops the banging about of the ball. When Hacker comes on, Gooch drives him straight for 6 with hardly any follow-through to put the 150 up. Or, if you like, to complete 64 runs in five and a half overs; for it is the astonishing arithmetic of this innings that is beginning to rivet us more than the strokes that are producing it. Scoring strokes follow in such rapid succession that it is becoming hard to appreciate one properly before it is overtaken by the next. Out of one corner of my eye I see that Gooch isn't far from his century; out of the other I'm watching the arc of the ball as it clears the sightscreen again. He fails to reach three figures by as many runs, when he tries to pull Mackintosh once more and is caught by French. But 97 in 94 minutes, with a couple of 6s and fourteen 4s, has been a powerful send-off to Australia for Graham Gooch.

There are 10 overs to be played and Essex still need 44 to win. It will be up to McEwan now, the experienced hand, a Wisden Cricketer of the Year. But it is nine-teen-year-old Lilley who carries on from where Gooch left off, and the South African plays downstage as supporting cast. Shirt buttoned at the cuffs under a sleeveless sweater, bushy hair tufting in the breeze he's creating himself, the young man takes leave of all modesty when he finds himself in the leading role. Twice in one over he leaps out to Doshi and drives him for 6. Then he pulls and hooks Mackintosh's seamers with abandon, as though he's never heard of pacing yourself, as though some devil says he must finish this match in every over bowled or perish in the attempt. He goes to meet all the attackers like that most famous picture of Victor Trumper, legs splayed in full stride, bat high behind his head, eyes and nose pointed sharply at the ball. This is his posture when he hits the most remarkable blow of the match, a 6 off Mackintosh that soars high over mid-off, is still rising when it crosses the boundary, and makes half a dozen people jump when it lands in the top of the West Wing stand. Even the Notts supporters, who have been pretty dumbfounded for an hour, can't fore-bear to cheer at that. They are watching a fiction in real life, the stuff that boys' comics used to thrive on when Rockfist Rogan was the Thursday hero and somebody's loyal tribesman on the North-west Frontier cracked skulls with a piece of timber that he called Clicky Ba.

Young Lilley gets his century after 123 minutes at the crease, having hit four 6s and nine 4s. There are still 5 overs left, but Essex need only one more run to win by 9 wickets. Sentimentality is not allowed to intrude. It is McEwan who scores that single, and Lilley remains 100 not out. This will have been one of the more remarkable victories of the season, and I am still dazed by its climax when the players have walked across the grass for the last time this year, ascended the pavilion steps with a scrunching of studs, and disappeared into their dressing rooms. I had expected to pass this last day pensively, as a drawn match and the 1978 season slipped away. Instead it has been so eventful, so rousing at the end, that there has been little time to reflect. The greyness of Trent Bridge, at a quarter to six and close of play, is caused by the weather and nothing else. As we who have watched stand up and stretch, take a last look round and very slowly depart, the sadness that all's done now is very small, comfortably borne in the being fulfilled. And, my word, there's a new name to keep an eye on next season.

## NOTTINGHAMSHIRE — *First Innings*

| | |
|---|---|
| P. A. TODD c Hardie b East | 59 |
| R. E. DEXTER lbw Lever | 1 |
| D. W. RANDALL c Gooch b East | 86 |
| C. E. B. RICE c Hardie b Acfield | 13 |
| M. J. SMEDLEY c Fletcher b East | 1 |
| B. N. FRENCH c and b Acfield | 1 |
| K. MACKINTOSH not out | 23 |
| P. J. HACKER c Gooch b East | 0 |
| K. COOPER c Fletcher b Acfield | 1 |
| M. E. ALLBROOK not out | 1 |
| Extras (lb 7, w 1, nb 6) | 14 |
| | |
| Total (for 8, declared) | 200 |

Fall of wickets: 2, 140, 167, 172, 173, 177, 178, 179.
Did not bat: D. R. Doshi.
Bowling: LEVER 20–4–50–1; TURNER 21–5–52–0; EAST 24–7–51–4; ACFIELD 17–6–33–3.

### *Second Innings*

| | |
|---|---|
| P. A. TODD b Acfield | 33 |
| R. E. DEXTER c Fletcher b East | 9 |
| D. W. RANDALL b East | 0 |

C. E. B. RICE c McEwan b Acfield — 3
M. J. SMEDLEY not out — 48
B. N. FRENCH c and b East — 30
K. S. MACKINTOSH not out — 13
Extras (b 2, lb 3, nb 2) — 7

Total (for 5, declared) — 143

Fall of wickets: 38, 41, 43, 60, 118.
Bowling: LEVER 7–1–19–0; TURNER 6–1–11–0; ACFIELD 19–3–43–2; EAST 18.2–3–63–3.

## ESSEX—*First Innings*

G. A. GOOCH c Todd b Cooper — 0
A. W. LILLEY c Rice b Doshi — 22
K. S. MCEWAN c Cooper b Doshi — 28
R. E. EAST c and b Cooper — 13
K. W. R. FLETCHER not out — 11
B. R. HARDIE c Smedley b Doshi — 6
K. R. PONT c Rice b Doshi — 0
S. TURNER c Smedley b Cooper — 3
N. SMITH not out — 32
Extras (b 4, lb 3) — 7

Total (for 7, declared) — 122

Fall of wickets: 0, 50, 54, 65, 72, 72, 75.
Did not bat: D. L. Acfield, J. K. Lever.
Bowling: COOPER 10–2–55–3; DOSHI 15–6–28–4; ALLBROOK 7–1–18–0; HACKER 1–0–14–0.

## *Second Innings*

G. A. GOOCH c French b Mackintosh — 97
A. W. LILLEY not out — 100
K. S. MCEWAN not out — 18
Extras (b 2, lb 4, w 1) — 7

Total (for 1) — 222

Fall of wicket: 159.

Bowling: COOPER 6–1–22–0; HACKER 5–0–37–0; DOSHI 12–1–67–0; ALLBROOK 5–1–42–0; MACKINTOSH 6.5–0–47–1.

Umpires: D. Oslear and K. Palmer.

Essex (15 points) beat Nottinghamshire (5 points) by nine wickets.